Grandpappy's Recipes for Hard Times

Robert Wayne Atkins, P.E.
(Grandpappy)

Simple Recipes Using Ingredients
Commonly Found in Many Kitchen Pantries.

A Wide Variety of Delicious Recipes
that Would Be Useful
During an Economic Depression
When Few Financial and/or Food Resources Are Available
or After a Natural or Manmade Disaster
that Disrupts Commerce.

For more information please visit: https://www.grandpappy.org

Grandpappy's Recipes for Hard Times
Robert Wayne Atkins, P.E. (Grandpappy)

Copyright © 2011, 2015 by Robert Wayne Atkins, P.E. All rights reserved. No part of this book may be used or reproduced in any manner without the written permission of the author except for brief quotes that are included as part of a review article. For additional information contact the author by email at: RobertWayneAtkins@hotmail.com

First Edition published by Grandpappy, Inc.

A Wide Variety of Delicious Recipes
that Would Be Useful During an Economic Depression
When Few Financial and/or Food Resources Are Available
or After a Natural or Manmade Disaster that Disrupts Commerce.

ISBN: 978-0-9837933-1-1

Printed in the United States of America.
10 9 8 7 6 5 4

Preface to

Grandpappy's Recipes for Hard Times

In June of the year 1975 my wife and I, plus our three preschool age children, lived in a tent on twelve acres of wilderness real estate we had purchased that was located deep in the backwoods of Maine. Each day we cooked our meals over a campfire. This was fun to do for a short period of time. However, as the weeks stretched into months the novelty quickly wore off and my entire family become disgusted at having to eat the same basic food again and again and again. This is referred to as "appetite fatigue" and unless it has actually happened to you then you will probably underestimate how depressing it can be.

In late November of the year 1975 we returned to civilization and we once again began living a common ordinary civilized life. However, those six months I spent in a hostile wilderness environment deep in the backwoods of Maine taught me a multitude of very valuable life lessons. For example:

1. Food is extremely important to your survival.
2. If you eat the same basic food items again and again then appetite fatigue will get the best of you.
3. To avoid appetite fatigue a person needs some very simple but practical recipes that will allow him or her to prepare an interesting and delicious variety of meals using the same basic food items.

Therefore I began diligently looking for simple recipes that could produce delightful results using the absolute minimum number of basic ordinary food items. I quickly discovered that ordinary simple food can be made absolutely delicious if it is properly prepared.

I also discovered that the vast majority of the recipes in almost every cookbook that I bought were based on the following three assumptions:

1. Your primary objective is to prepare one recipe or one meal at a time.
2. You can afford to invest a lot of money in a wide assortment of basic ingredients for that one recipe.
3. Those recipe ingredients can be easily found at your local grocery store.

Since I had lived for six months in the wilderness of Maine I knew the above three assumptions were not valid for a family that was experiencing hard times.

As the years passed I continued to add to my original collection of basic simple recipes. For the past 35 years I have been diligently searching for simple recipes that produce delicious results.

However, I also knew that under hardship conditions a family would need to supplement their meals with wild edible plants and wild game meat. Therefore I began experimenting with a variety of wild edible plants and wild game meats. I quickly discovered that almost 95% of the wild plants listed in "survival manuals" do not grow everywhere. And when they can be found there is usually only just enough for one small meal. Therefore I began focusing my attention on a few wild plants that are extremely common, and that grow in abundance, and that most people can easily recognize. Those are the wild edible plants that are included in this book, such as white oak acorns. This cookbook explains how to identify, process, and prepare white oak acorns using a wide variety of different acorn recipes.

Some wild game animals are relatively small and they will only provide enough meat for one meal. Other wild game animals could feed you for an entire week. And some wild game animals have enough meat to last several weeks. Therefore a family would need to have a reliable method of preserving that meat for future consumption without having to rely on a food freezer or canning jars. That is why I began experimenting with a variety of different meat jerky recipes. I eventually developed my own jerky recipe that will work with any type of meat. My meat jerky recipe is in this cookbook.

I also knew that the summer fruit and berry harvest season is relatively short and that a family would need to store those fruits and berries for consumption during the cold winter months. That is the reason I developed the Pemmican recipe in this cookbook. My Pemmican recipe allows you to combine your fruits and berries with your meat jerky to make a "delicious granola bar" that is a complete nutritious meal all by itself.

I also realized that the time may come when a family may not be able to conveniently replenish their food supplies at their local grocery store for one reason or another. Therefore I developed my own special recipes on how to convert ordinary vegetables that you can grow in a home garden into the food items you would normally buy from a store. For example, this cookbook contains recipes that explain how to convert fresh tomatoes into tomato sauce, pizza sauce, spaghetti sauce, Mexican salsa, and catsup. This cookbook also explains how to extract the sucrose sugar from ordinary sugar beets to create your own sugar and sugar syrup.

Depending on what type of emergency food supplies you now have in storage you may need more than one cookbook. For example:

1. If you have a significant investment in dehydrated and freeze-dried foods then your family really needs a special cookbook that is dedicated to these unique types of foods.
2. If you have a huge inventory of hundreds of different types of foods and spices and flavorings and wines then your family really needs a conventional cookbook that explains how to provide unique meals using a multitude of different ingredients in each recipe.
3. If you have less that one-hundred different food items in storage and those food items are common ordinary foods then your family really needs this cookbook.

Even if you currently fall into category one or two above, you will eventually consume all your stored foods. When that happens your family may be reduced to eating the same common ordinary foods that all the rest of us already eat on a regular basis. In that situation this cookbook could become extremely important in maximizing your family's eating pleasure at the dining table.

Now let me tell you what this cookbook does **not** contain. It does not contain any microwave oven recipes. It does not contain a lot of recipes for hamburger, or fish, or vegetables. This cookbook only contains a few very basic simple recipes for each type of food.

However, this cookbook does go into great depth on the more important food items, such as white rice, flour (or wheat berries), cornmeal, and acorns. This cookbook also contains instructions on how to process a variety of common wild game animals so you can successfully add them to your meals. This cookbook will also help you to identify and prepare the most common wild plants when they are in season, such as dandelions and kudzu. Finally, it will help you to avoid vitamin deficiency problems by providing nutritional data on several wild plants, such as the common ordinary pine needle (vitamin C).

In addition to food recipes this cookbook also contains my homemade wine recipes and my homemade beer recipe. In my opinion my basic wine recipe will consistently produce delicious wine even if you don't have the special wine making chemicals and yeasts specified in traditional wine recipes. However, my beer recipe is only based on three years of homebrewing and I was not able to create a beer that tasted *exactly* like a true American light beer. However, my beer recipe does produce a pretty good light beer and it would be an excellent starting position for someone who wanted to create the perfect American light beer and who wanted to continue where I left off.

I am sometimes asked which recipes are my personal favorites. My seven favorite recipes are:

1. Bacon plus Scrambled Eggs with Cheese on page 4.
2. Sausage and Cheese Biscuits on page 27.
3. Pot Luck Pie on page 16.
4. Spaghetti with Meatballs on page 19.
5. Hamburger, Rice, and Eggs on page 15.
6. Peanut Butter Cookies with Optional Chocolate Chips on page 54.
7. Fantastic Fudge on page 53.

Respectfully,
Robert Wayne Atkins, P.E. (Grandpappy)
July 1, 2011

Table of Contents

Chapter   **Page**

Section One: Introduction
1. Introduction to Grandpappy's Recipes and a Temperature Conversion Table 1
2. Some Practical Cooking Advice 3

Section Two: Homemade Items
3. Useful Homemade Items When Store Bought Items Might Not Be Available 5
4. Grandpappy's Tomato Sauce, Pizza Sauce, Spaghetti Sauce, Mexican Salsa, and Catsup 7
5. Grandpappy's Homemade Sugar Recipe 9

Section Three: Vegetables
6. Beans 11
7. Potatoes 12
8. White Rice 13

Section Four: Meat
9. Meat Recipes 17

Section Five: Bread
10. Introduction to Breads and Yeast 20
11. Yeast Breads 22
12. Bread without Yeast (No Eggs Required) 25
13. Sourdough Bread (No Eggs Required) 28
14. Bagels, Pretzels, Crackers, Chips, and Cheese Snacks (No Eggs Required) 31
15. Breads Made from Oat Flour and Rice Flour (No Eggs Required) 33

Section Six: Cornmeal
16. Cornmeal Recipes (No Eggs Required) 34

Section Seven: Wheat Berries
17. Wheat Berry Recipes 36

Section Eight: Desserts
18. Grandpappy's Delicious Homemade Ice Cream using Instant Powdered Milk 40
19. Cakes and Frostings (No Eggs Required) 41
20. Cookies (No Eggs Required) 44
21. Pies and Cobblers 48
22. Candy and Fudge 51
23. Sweet Treats 54

Section Nine: Edible Wild Plants and Nuts
24. Edible Wild Plants: Cattails, Pine Needles, Dandelions, Poke Sallet, Kudzu, Etc. 58
25. Acorns 64
26. Hickory Nuts 74

Section Ten: Fish and Wild Game
27 Fish 76
28 Aquatic and Land Creatures 77
29 Wild Game Recipes 78

Section Eleven: Meat Jerky and Pemmican
30 Meat Jerky 83
31 Grandpappy's Pemmican Recipe: A Native American Indian Survival Food 85

Section Twelve: Beverages
32 Hot and Cold Beverages 89
33 Introduction to Alcoholic Beverages 91
34 Grandpappy's Homemade Beer Recipes 93
35 Grandpappy's Homemade Wine Recipes 97

   Index 102
   About the Author 106

Page Number of Each Recipe

Useful Homemade Items

Recipe	Page
Useful Substitutions	1
Quantity Conversion Table	1
Salt and Pepper	1
Cooking Temperature Conversion Chart	2
Practical Cooking Tips	3
Baking Soda and Baking Powder	3
Instant Nonfat Dry Milk	3
Bacon	4
Eggs: Fresh, Hard Boiled, Scrambled	4
Baking Powder	5
Self-Rising Flour	5
Homemade Bisquick Mix	5
Homemade Sweetened Condensed Milk	5
Sour Cream	5
Mayonnaise (Recipe One)	5
Mayonnaise (Recipe Two)	5
Smooth Peanut Butter	6
Fruit Pectin (Use in Jam and Jelly Recipes)	6
Homemade Liquid Hop Yeast	6
Hop Yeast	6
Homemade Tomato Sauce, Spaghetti Sauce	7
Homemade Pizza Sauce, Salsa, and Catsup	8
Homemade Sugar from Sugar Beets	9

Vegetables

Dry Beans	11
Refried Beans	11
Potato Cakes	12
Hash Brown Potatoes	12
Potato Chips	12
White Rice General Instructions	13
Rice Flour	13
Basic Burrito	13
Rice and Beans	13
Feathered Rice	13
Baked Rice	14

Recipe	Page
Mexican or Spanish Rice	14
Indian Rice	14
Herb Flavored Rice	14
Rice Pilaf	15
Rice-A-Roni	15
Stuffed Grape (or Cabbage) Leaves	15
Hamburger, Rice, and Scrambled Eggs	15
Fried Leftover Rice	16
Sweet Leftover Rice	16
Pot Luck Pie	16
Warm Rice and Tuna	16
Chilled Rice and Tuna Salad	16
Chilled Rice, Tuna, and Fruit Salad	16

Meat

Recipe	Page
Chicken Fried Steak	17
Southern Fried Chicken	17
Northern Fried Chicken	17
Chicken Parts	17
Chicken and Dumplings	17
Chicken Broth	17
Beef Broth	18
Shish Kabobs (Kebabs)	18
Roast Beef Hash	18
Beans and Wieners	18
Pigs in a Blanket	18
Tuna Casserole	18
Salmon (or Mackerel) Patties	19
Spaghetti with Meat Balls	19
Chili with Beans	19

Bread

Recipe	Page
Yeast Preparation Instructions	20
Optional Bread Crust Variations	20
Liquid Substitutions	21
Optional Ingredients	21

Page Number of Each Recipe

Recipe	Page
Wheat Flour and Wheat Berries	21
100% Whole Wheat Loaf Bread	22
100% Whole Wheat French Bread	22
Sandwich Buns	22
Hard Rolls	23
Wheat Rolls	23
Whole Wheat Crescent Rolls	23
English Muffins	23
English Muffin Loaf	24
Pita Bread	24
Bread on the Grill	24
Pizza Dough	24
Pancakes (No Eggs)	25
Flour Tortillas	25
Baking Powder Biscuits	25
Camp Biscuits or Biscuit Twists	26
Salt-Rising Bread (Recipe One)	26
Salt-Rising Bread (Recipe Two)	26
Irish Soda Bread	27
Sausage and Cheese Biscuits	27
Choctaw Indian Fry Bread	27
Sourdough Starter using a Fresh Potato	28
Sourdough Starter using Instant Potatoes	28
Sourdough Starter using Honey	28
Sourdough Starter Water Base	29
Sourdough Starter Buttermilk Base	29
Sourdough Starter Milk Base	29
Sourdough Loaf Bread	29
Sourdough French Bread	30
Sourdough Biscuits	30
Sourdough Pancakes	30
Whole Wheat Bagels	31
Whole Wheat Pretzels	31
Whole Wheat Crackers	31
Graham Crackers	31
Whole Wheat Chips	32
Cheddar Cheese Crackers	32

Recipe	Page
Cheese Wafers	32
Oat Flour Instructions	33
Rice Flour Instructions	33
Oatmeal Bread	33
Three-Grain Bread	33

Cornmeal

Corn Bread	34
Corn Tortillas, Corn Chips, Taco Shells	34
Hush Puppies	34
Corn Pone	34
Pioneer Hoe Cakes	34
Cornmeal Mush and Polenta	35
Corn Dogs	35
Parched Corn and Cornmeal	35

Wheat Berries

Wheat Berry Introduction	36
Wheat Sprouts	36
Wheat Berry or Cracked Wheat Cereal	36
Wheat Berry Cereal (Thermos Method)	37
Wheat Berry Cereal (Microwave)	37
Chilled Wheat Berry Salad	37
Popped Wheat	37
Sautéed Sprouts	37
Simmered Sprouts	37
Wheat Berry Nutritional Information	38

Desserts

Grandpappy's Delicious Ice Cream	40
Decorative Icing Suggestions	41
Apple Cake	41
Shortcake	41
Hard Cake	41
Easy Chocolate Cake	41

Table of Contents

Page Number of Each Recipe

Recipe	Page
Basic Chocolate Cake	42
Confectioners Frosting I	42
Confectioners Frosting II	42
Confectioners Frosting III	42
Confectioners Butter Frosting	42
Creamy Chocolate Frosting	42
Peanut Butter Chocolate Frosting	43
Caramel Icing I	43
Caramel Icing II	43
Granulated Sugar Icing	43
Granulated Sugar Topping	43
Cinnamon Sugar Sprinkle	43
Cookies Introduction (No Eggs)	44
Basic Cookie Recipe and Sugar Cookies	44
Shortbread Cookies	44
Fruit Preserves Cookies	44
Crescent Cookies	44
Welch Scones	45
Dutch Cookies	45
Swedish Butter Cookies	45
Scottish Butter Cookies	45
Honey Cookies	46
Honey Wheat Cookies	46
Pecan Sandies	46
Snowball Cookies I	46
Snowball Cookies II	46
Oatmeal Cookies	47
Boiled Oatmeal Cookies	47
Decorative Pie Crust Patterns	48
9-Inch Pie Crust	48
Rich Southern Pastry	48
Easy Pie Crust	48
Graham Cracker Pie Crust	49
Fruit Preserves Pie	49
Berry or Fruit Pie	49
Shoo Fly Pie	49
Fruit Cobber (using Fresh Fruit)	49
Fruit Cobbler (using Canned Fruit)	50
Blueberry (Huckleberry) Crisp	50
Fried Pies	50
Peanut Butter Candy Roll	51
Peanut Butter Candy I	51
Peanut Butter Candy II	51
Peanut Butter Candy III	51
Whole Wheat Peanut Butter Candy	51
Easy Peanut Butter Fudge	52
Peanut Butter Fudge	52
Chocolate Fudge	52
Creamy Butter Fudge	52
Extra Creamy Fudge	52
Cocoa Fudge	52
Fantastic Fudge (Every Time)	53
Caramels	53
Butterscotch Candy	53
Peanut Butter Cookies with One Egg	54
Peanut Butter Balls	54
Cinnamon Rolls	54
Icing for Cinnamon Rolls	54
Homemade Marshmallows	55
Caramel Syrup	55
Popcorn	55
Caramel Popcorn	55
Basic Pudding	56
Chocolate Pudding	56
Kool Aid Pudding (or Pie Glaze)	56
Pioneer Pudding	56
Chilled Blueberry and Mint Rice Pudding	56
Warm Rice Pudding	57
Chilled Rice Sundae	57
Homemade Granola	57
Chewy Granola Bars	57
Corn Cob Jelly	57
Pear Preserves	57

Page Number of Each Recipe

Edible Wild Plants and Nuts

Recipe	Page
How to Identify Edible Wild Plants	58
Five-Step Safety Procedure	58
Berries	58
Cattails	58
Evergreen Needles	59
Pine Needle Juice	59
Clover: White, Yellow, Red	59
Daisy	59
Birch Juice	59
Inner Tree Bark	59
Dandelions	60
Dandelion Nutritional Information	60
Poke Sallet Weed	61
Kudzu Introduction	62
Kudzu Flower Tea	63
Kudzu Root Tea	63
Acorns Overview	64
Acorn Grits	70
Acorn Meal (or Acorn Flour)	70
Acorn Grits and Meal Substitutions	70
Indian Acorn Griddlecakes	70
Mexican Acorn Tortillas	70
Acorn Pemmican Tortillas	70
Pioneer Acorn Bread and Muffins	71
Pioneer Acorn Pancakes	71
Breakfast Acornmeal	71
Acorn and Corn Meal Mush	71
Acorn Bread	71
Glazed Acorn Treats	72
Acorn Cookies	72
Acorn Nutritional Information	73
Hickory Nuts Introduction	74
Mother Marsh's Hickory Nut Cake	74
Hickory Nut Pie	74
Hickory Nut Nutritional Information	75

Fish and Wild Game

Recipe	Page
Fish and Trout	76
Aquatic and Land Creatures	77
Wild Game: General Instructions	78
Armadillo	79
Beaver and Beaver Tail	79
Groundhog (Woodchuck)	79
Muskrat	79
Opossum	79
Porcupine	80
Rabbit	80
Raccoon	80
Squirrel	80
Bear and Bear Fat	81
Deer (Venison)	81
Campfire Cooking Instructions	81
Wild Game Stew	82
Meat Grinder and How to Grind Meat	82
Bone Marrow	82

Meat Jerky and Pemmican

Meat Jerky	83
Grandpappy's Pemmican Recipe	85

Beverages

Baby Formula (8 Ounce Bottle)	89
Electrolyte Beverage (Gatorade, Pedialyte)	89
Hot Chocolate or Chocolate Milk	89
Chocolate Milkshake	89
Peanut Butter Milkshake	89
Chilled Rice Beverage or Milkshake	89
Russian Tea	90
Clover Tea	90
Alcohol Introduction	91
Grandpappy's Homemade Beer Recipes	93
Grandpappy's Homemade Wine Recipes	97

Chapter One

Introduction to Grandpappy's Recipes and Some Useful Substitutions

Preface to all the Recipes: Don't be afraid to modify my recipes and use slightly different amounts of the listed ingredients. Or you can experiment and substitute other ingredients. That is what good cooks do -- they find the right combination of ingredients in the right quantities that are pleasing to the taste. A little change can produce exciting and delightful results. Too much change can ruin a recipe.

When I was born in 1949 I didn't know anything about cooking. Therefore, with only a few exceptions, most of my recipes were acquired by reading recipe books or by watching someone else prepare food. All I did was take notes. Frequently I made minor adjustments to the ingredients in a recipe to please my own taste requirements. Therefore you may discover that some of my recipes are very similar to ones you are already familiar with. I make no apologies. Cooking is both an art and a science. And I practice both.

Abbreviations Used in All the Recipes

| tsp. = teaspoon | tbsp. = tablespoon | oz. = ounce | lb. = pound |

Quantity Conversion Table

| 1 tsp. = 1/3 tbsp. | 1 cup = 8 ounces | 1 quart = 2 pints |
| 1 tbsp. = 1/2 ounce | 1 pint = 2 cups | 1 gallon = 4 quarts |

Useful Substitutions

1 tsp. baking powder = 1/4 tsp. baking soda + 1/2 tsp. cream tartar + 1/4 tsp. cornstarch

1 tsp. baking powder = 1/3 tsp. baking soda + 1/2 tsp. cream tartar

1 cup butter = 1 cup shortening + 1/2 tsp. salt

1 tbsp. oil = 1 tbsp. melted shortening (or lard)

1 cup corn syrup = 1 cup honey = 1 cup sugar + 1/2 cup of the liquid used in the recipe

1 cup buttermilk = 1 cup milk + 1 tbsp. vinegar (or lemon juice)

1 cup nonfat milk = 1/3 cup nonfat dry milk + 1 cup water

1 cup whole milk = 1/3 cup nonfat dry milk + 1 cup water + 2 tbsp. melted butter

1 cup whole milk = 1/2 cup evaporated milk + 1/2 cup water

1 cup sugar = 1 cup corn syrup (decrease recipe liquid by 1/4 cup)

1 cup sugar = 1 cup honey (decrease recipe liquid by 1/4 cup)

1 oz. unsweetened chocolate = 3 tbsp. cocoa + 1 tbsp. shortening

Salt and Pepper

Some recipes specify the addition of salt and/or pepper to the other ingredients in the recipe (such as Salt-Rising Bread). If the recipe specifically recommends salt and/or pepper then add the recommended amounts as you prepare the food. However, if the recipe does not specify salt or pepper then you should allow each member of your family to add salt and pepper to the food on their own plates at the dining table. This will give each person the opportunity to season his or her own food as he or she prefers.

Cooking Temperature Conversion Chart
Degrees Fahrenheit (°F) to Degrees Centigrade (°C)
Centigrade is also called Celsius

Equation: °C = (°F - 32°) x (5/9)

100°F	=	37.8°C
125°F	=	51.7°C
150°F	=	65.6°C
175°F	=	79.4°C
200°F	=	93.3°C
225°F	=	107.2°C
250°F	=	121.1°C
275°F	=	135.0°C
300°F	=	148.9°C
325°F	=	162.8°C
350°F	=	176.7°C
375°F	=	190.6°C
400°F	=	204.4°C
425°F	=	218.3°C
450°F	=	232.2°C

Chapter Two

Some Practical Cooking Advice

Practical Cooking Tips

1. When available, use shortening to grease baking pans. If you use butter, margarine, or oils then they will be absorbed into the dough more quickly.
2. If a glass pan is used for baking then reduce the recommended oven temperature by 25 degrees.
3. Do **not** use aluminum pots when cooking foods that are high in acids, such as tomatoes. The high acidic foods will interact with the aluminum and introduce unacceptable unusual flavors.
4. Instant potatoes work well as a thickener for homemade stews.
5. Vegetables that grow above ground should be boiled with **no** cover on the cook pot.
6. If fresh vegetables need to be soaked then do so **before** slicing in order to retain as much of their nutritional value as possible.
7. Cut meat across the grain before cooking to make it easier to eat after cooking.

Baking Soda and Baking Powder

Baking soda is pure sodium bicarbonate.

Baking powder is baking soda plus cream of tartar plus a starch (such as corn starch).

If you need to, you may use baking powder in place of baking soda in a recipe but you should **not** use baking soda in place of baking powder in a recipe.

Two Recipes for Baking Powder

Baking powder or yeast will cause your bread to rise when you bake it.
But both baking powder and yeast have relatively short shelf lives.
The good news is that you can make your own baking powder using either of the following two recipes:

1 tsp. baking powder = 1/4 tsp. baking soda + 1/2 tsp. cream tartar + 1/4 tsp. cornstarch

1 tsp. baking powder = 1/3 tsp. baking soda + 1/2 tsp. cream tartar (no cornstarch)

When the cream of tartar is combined with the baking soda a chemical reaction takes place and the shelf life of the resulting baking powder is only a few months. Therefore it is best to make just enough baking powder when you need it so that it will always be fresh and very active.

Instant Nonfat Dry Milk

The flavor and texture of instant nonfat dry milk can be improved by mixing it with the proper quantity of very hot water and then chilling it overnight in the refrigerator. This gives the powder a chance to completely dissolve and blend with the water.

The flavor of instant milk can be further enhanced by adding approximately 12 ounces of normal milk (whole milk or condensed milk or evaporated milk) to approximately one-gallon of the chilled powdered milk and then mixing it all together thoroughly. In other words, add about 10% real milk to 90% powdered milk to improve its flavor.

Instant nonfat dry powdered milk will retain most of its nutritional value for at least 20 years, if it is stored in a cool and dry environment. However, as it ages it gradually loses its flavor.

The flavor of old powdered milk can be enhanced by mixing it with the proper quantity of hot water. Then add a little vanilla extract (or a little sugar) and let it chill for a few hours in the refrigerator before serving. (Note: Another obvious solution would be to add a little chocolate flavoring.)

The gradual decline in the flavor of old powdered milk will not be noticed by *most* people if it is used as a dry ingredient in a baking recipe instead of drinking it as a beverage.

Bacon

Although you can fry bacon in a skillet, the best way to cook bacon is in the oven. Place strips of bacon on a two-piece broiler pan so the bacon grease can collect in the lower half of the pan. Bake at 450°F in the center of the oven. Turn the bacon over after 10 minutes. The bacon will be crisp in about 15 to 20 minutes. The thickness of the bacon determines the time required to cook the bacon, so you must check the bacon as it cooks to avoid burning it. Remove each strip of bacon when it is done. Drain the bacon on a paper towel before serving. (Note: Before the bacon grease hardens, pour the warm bacon grease into a suitable storage container with a lid. You may then use it as needed in other recipes. For example, add a little bacon grease to your beans when you cook them to give them a unique flavor.)

Fresh Eggs

You can check the quality of eggs by placing them in a bowl of cold water. If they float then they are **not** fresh and they should **not** be used.

Hard Boiled Eggs: Put fresh eggs in water and bring to a boil. After the water starts to boil, wait at least seven minutes. Turn off the heat and put a lid on the pot but leave the eggs in the hot water for another five minutes. Then pour off the hot water and cover the eggs with cool water. Wait two minutes. Crack the egg shell by gently hitting it against a counter top at several different places on the exterior of the egg. Peel off the egg shell using the thin inner membrane that has separated from the boiled egg and is now between the egg and the exterior shell.

Scrambled Eggs: Break the eggs by hitting them gently against the inside flat bottom of a non-stick skillet. Discard the egg shells (or add the crushed egg shells to your compost pile). Thoroughly mix the yokes and egg whites together using a long plastic fork or a long plastic forked spoon. Turn on the heat below the skillet to low or medium-low. Continuously stir the eggs while they are cooking. As they cook you should scrape the eggs off the bottom of the skillet and mix them with the rest of the eggs in the skillet. Do not let the eggs stick to the bottom of the skillet and burn. The most important thing is to continuously stir the eggs while they are cooking. Continuous stirring is not intermittent stirring. The eggs should be completely done in about 5 to 7 minutes. If the eggs are done sooner than 5 minutes then you are using too much heat and you need to reduce the heat next time. If the eggs take longer than 7 minutes then you will need to increase the heat a little the next time you scramble eggs.

Scrambled Eggs with Cheese: After mixing the yokes and egg whites together in the bottom of the skillet, add one rounded tablespoon of shredded cheddar cheese per egg (either mild or sharp cheddar cheese). Thoroughly mix the cheese with the eggs. Then turn on the heat to low or medium-low and follow the above instructions.

Scrambled Eggs with Milk: Add one teaspoon of milk per egg and follow the above instructions. Do not add both cheese and milk to the eggs. Select one or the other.

Why Are Some of My Recipes Egg Free?

I love eggs and I use eggs in a variety of the recipes I prepare on a regular basis. However, I am aware that fresh eggs might not be available under hardship conditions. Therefore I have been on the lookout for good recipes that don't require eggs for many years. Good "no egg recipes" are not easy to find.

Under hardship conditions you may have all the other necessary ingredients to prepare a recipe but you don't have any fresh eggs. And a quick trip to the local store may not be an option.

If you just omit the eggs from the original recipe then you normally end up with a culinary disaster that your family will not eat. The basic recipe needs to be modified and other ingredients added to serve the original function of the eggs.

In you should find yourself in a situation where you don't have fresh eggs then my "no egg recipes" can be used to produce delightful results to satisfy your family's desire for a tasty and nutritional meal.

My "no egg recipes" would also be useful for anyone who is allergic to eggs.

Chapter Three

Useful Homemade Items
When Store Bought Items Might Not Be Available

Baking Powder (from McCormick's Cream of Tartar Label)

| 1/2 tsp. cream of tartar | 1/4 tsp. baking soda | 1/4 tsp. cornstarch |

Thoroughly blend all ingredients. Then use exactly like baking powder. (Note: If you don't have cornstarch then increase the baking soda to 1/3 tsp.)

Self-Rising Flour

| 1 cup flour | 1/2 tbsp. baking powder | 1/2 tsp. salt |

May be used in any recipe that specifies self-rising flour.

Homemade Bisquick Mix

| 3 cups flour | 1 tbsp. baking powder | 1 tsp. salt |
| 4 tsp. granulated sugar | 1/2 cup shortening | |

Mix everything together and use in any recipe that requires Bisquick Ready Mix.

Homemade Sweetened Condensed Milk

| 1 cup instant nonfat dry milk | 1/3 cup boiling water |
| 2/3 cup granulated sugar | 1/4 cup butter, melted (optional) |

If the optional butter is omitted, then increase the water to 1/2 cup and increase the sugar to 3/4 cup. Combine all ingredients and mix until smooth. Store this milk in the refrigerator for up to 5 days.

Homemade Sour Cream

| 1 cup instant nonfat dry milk | 1/2 cup warm water | 1 tbsp. vinegar or lemon juice |

Add the dry milk to the warm water in a bowl and stir until completely dissolved. Add the vinegar a few drops at a time and continue stirring. Place in the refrigerator for six-hours and the mixture will thicken.

Mayonnaise (Recipe One)

| 2 egg yolks | 2 cups salad oil | 1/8 tsp. cayenne |
| 1 tsp. dry mustard | 3 tbsp. lemon juice | |

Mix egg yolks with dry mustard and cayenne. Stir in lemon juice. Beat in 1/2 cup salad oil a few drops at a time. Then beat in another 1 1/2 cups of oil more rapidly.

Mayonnaise (Recipe Two)

| 3 eggs | 1 cup cream | 1/2 cup sugar |
| 1/2 tsp. mustard | 1/2 tbsp. vinegar | 1/2 tsp. salt |

Beat eggs. Add cream, sugar, and mustard. Mix well. Very gradually add the vinegar. Cook in a double boiler until thick (do **not** boil). Add salt after the mixture cools.

Smooth Peanut Butter

| 1 cup roasted shelled peanuts | 1.5 tsp. oil | 1/4 tsp. salt |

Note: Omit the salt if you are using salted peanuts.
Note: The oil may be peanut oil, or olive oil, or vegetable oil. The flavor of the oil will be present in the finished peanut butter.
Note: If you have fresh unroasted peanuts then remove the peanuts from their shells, rub off and discard the paper thin pink skins, place the peanuts on a cookie sheet and roast in an oven at 300°F for 12 minutes. Allow the peanuts to cool before using.
Directions: Place the roasted peanuts, the oil, and the salt in a blender and secure the lid. Blend until the mixture becomes spreadable. If necessary, add a few more drops of oil. If necessary, stop the blender and scrape the mixture off the sides of the blender to the bottom of the blender, and then continue blending. Use the peanut butter immediately or store it in an air-tight container in the refrigerator. If the oil separates during storage and rises to the top of the mixture then stir it back into the peanut butter before using.
Option: For **crunchy** peanut butter, stir in 1/8 cup of finely chopped roasted peanuts after blending.

Fruit Pectin (Used in jam and jelly recipes)

| 10 or 12 green, hard, sour apples (not yet ripe) |

Do **not** use ripe apples. Do not peel the apples. Cut the apples into quarters. Do not remove the seeds. Place in a large pot and add just enough water to barely cover the apples. Cover the pot and simmer on very low heat until the apples are fully cooked. Stir every twenty-minutes. When the mixture looks like runny applesauce it is done. Place a strainer or colander over another clean pot. Place a clean cloth inside the strainer. Pour the hot applesauce mixture into the cloth covered strainer so it can drip through into the large pot underneath. It will take several hours for the mixture to drain through the clean cloth. The slimy thick liquid in the pot is the fruit pectin. Refrigerate or freeze it until it is needed in a recipe.
How to Use: Substitute the above apple pectin in any recipe that requires a box of fruit pectin (about 1.75 ounces) by using 3 tablespoons apple pectin with 4 tablespoons sugar.

Homemade Liquid Hop Yeast

1 ounce hops	4 tsp. brown sugar	1 cup smooth mashed potatoes
2 cups flour	4 tsp. salt	2 quarts water (No Chlorine)

Early in the day, boil one ounce of hops in two quarts of water for thirty minutes. Strain and let the liquid cool to the warmth of fresh milk. Put in an earthen crock or bowl. Add 4 teaspoons each of salt and brown sugar. Now beat 2 cups of flour with part of the liquid and add to the remainder of liquid, mixing well. Set the mixture in a warm place for 3 days. Then add 1 cup smooth, mashed potatoes. Keep near the range in a warm place and stir frequently until it is well fermented. Place in a sterile, wide mouth jug or glass jar, and store in a cool place until ready to use. It will remain active for 2 months and improve with age. Use the same quantity as regular yeast but shake the jar well before using.

Hop Yeast

1 tsp. hops	1 tbsp. sugar	1 pint pure water (No Chlorine)
1 tbsp. flour	1 large potato, diced	1 glass bottle

Boil potato and add hops while boiling. Boil for 20 minutes. Strain and cool slightly. Then add flour and sugar. Bottle and cork tightly. The yeast will take about 24 hours to mature. Adding a maximum of 1 or 2 raisins (or currants) will speed up the process. This yeast will substitute for store bought yeast.

Chapter Three: Homemade Items

Chapter Four

Grandpappy's Homemade Tomato Sauce, Pizza Sauce, Spaghetti Sauce, Mexican Salsa, and Catsup Recipes Using Fresh Tomatoes

Introduction:
There is no universal recipe for making the "perfect" tomato sauce because different people have different taste preferences.

Sauce Thickness:
1. Tomato sauce can be made **thinner** by adding just a little water.
2. Tomato sauce can be made **thicker** by cooking it a little longer.

Sauce Cooking Time:
1. A shorter cooking time (one hour) will preserve more of the "fresh tomato" taste and yield a thinner sauce that still contains small pieces of tomato.
2. A medium cooking time (two hours) will gradually soften the tiny tomato pieces and create a smoother sauce.
3. A longer cooking time (3 to 4 hours) over very, very low heat will give all the ingredients in the sauce a chance to more thoroughly and completely blend together to create a fuller, richer taste. It will also result in a thicker sauce because more of the moisture will have been cooked off. If you prefer a thinner sauce you can always add a little water later to yield the sauce consistency you prefer.

Basic Tomato Sauce Ingredients (yields about 1.5 cups of pure tomato sauce):
2.5 pounds or about 5 ripe tomatoes of average size (or 2 pounds or 9 "Roma" plum size tomatoes) (Note: "Roma" tomatoes contain less water than other tomatoes).
2 tablespoons extra virgin olive oil (or 2 tablespoons of properly rendered melted animal fat).
1 teaspoon salt (you may use more or less salt depending on your salt preference).
1/3 teaspoon ground black pepper (you may omit the black pepper or use more or less pepper as you wish).

Optional Additional Ingredients To Make Spaghetti Sauce (yields 2 cups of spaghetti sauce):
1/3 cup green (or red or yellow) bell pepper, diced or grated, no seeds (you may omit the bell pepper if you wish).
1/3 cup onion, diced or grated (you may omit the onion if you don't like onions).
1 garlic clove, diced or grated (not a whole garlic) (or 1 teaspoon garlic salt or garlic powder).
1 teaspoon granulated sugar (or 2 teaspoons sugar beet water, or 1 grated carrot) (adds a sweet taste).
1/2 teaspoon basil (if you like the flavor of basil).
1/2 teaspoon thyme (if you like the flavor of thyme).
1/2 teaspoon parsley (if you like the flavor of parsley).
1/2 teaspoon oregano (if you like the flavor of oregano).

Cooking Directions:
1. Do **not** use an aluminum pot when cooking tomatoes. Any high acidic food, such as tomatoes, will interact with the aluminum and produce off flavors.
2. Fill a pot with water and bring it to a boil. Fill a large bowl with very, very cold water or ice water. Put the whole tomatoes in the boiling water for one-minute. Then immediately transfer the whole tomatoes to the bowl of very cold water using a slotted spoon. Wait for the tomatoes to cool so they can be handled with your hands. Then remove the skins. Dispose of the hot and cold water.

3. Cut the tomatoes into quarters from end to end. Scrape out and discard the seeds and the top center hard piece of the tomato.
4. Dice the tomatoes into very, very small pieces. The smaller the diced tomato pieces the more closely your final tomato sauce will look like canned tomato sauce. Or process the tomatoes on very low speed in an electric blender or food processor. Tomatoes processed using a blender will yield a final sauce that is almost identical in appearance to a canned tomato sauce.
5. Heat the olive oil in a non-stick sauce pan. If you are making spaghetti sauce or salsa then add the grated green bell pepper and the grated onion and heat for three minutes to give these flavors a chance to mix with the olive oil.
6. Add the finely diced tomatoes, the salt, and the black pepper. If appropriate, stir in the optional sugar.
7. If you are using garlic, or basil, or thyme, or parsley, or oregano, or carrot, then add them at this time. (You should have already rinsed them with clean water and minced them into tiny pieces or processed them in a blender.)
8. Add heat until you can hear the olive oil sizzling and then immediately reduce the heat to a very, very, very low simmer. Cover the sauce pan and cook between one-hour to four-hours depending on how thick you like your tomato sauce. Stir often while cooking (at least once every five or ten minutes).

Pizza Sauce:
Add the garlic, sugar, basil, thyme, and oregano but omit the bell pepper, the onion, and the parsley.
If available, add 2 teaspoons lemon juice.
Stir frequently and simmer until thick.
Follow the directions for making pizza dough in the bread section of these recipes.

Mexican Salsa:
Add the bell pepper, onion, and garlic but omit the sugar and omit the four herbs.
Add between 1/2 to 1 cup diced hot peppers with their seeds (jalapeno peppers or cayenne peppers).
Simmer for a total of 20 minutes, remove from the heat, allow the salsa to cool, and serve.

Catsup (or Ketchup):
Add the bell pepper, onion, and garlic but omit the sugar and omit the four herbs.
Add 3 tablespoons dark brown sugar (or granulated sugar).
Add 1/4 cup apple cider vinegar.
Add 1/2 teaspoon cinnamon.
Add 1/2 teaspoon paprika.
Simmer for two hours with a cover on the sauce pan stirring frequently. Then simmer for approximately one more hour without a cover on the sauce pan, stirring frequently, until the catsup thickens. Remove from heat and allow it to cool. As the catsup cools it will gradually get a little thicker but it will **not** be the same consistency as commercial catsup.

Chapter Four: Homemade Tomato Sauces

Chapter Five

Grandpappy's Homemade Sugar Recipe

Sugar (or Sucrose):
Sugar cane and sugar beets both produce the same type of sugar and it is called sucrose. Approximately 70% of the sugar (sucrose) consumed worldwide is produced from sugar cane and the remaining 30% is produced from sugar beets.

Historical Note:
In the late 1800s many American homesteads made their own sugar using sugar beets they grew on their own land. However, this practice was gradually abandoned when commercially produced cane sugar become widely available and affordable. Today only large commercial processing plants still make sugar from beets and that sugar is used in a variety of products, such as breakfast cereals. The commercial processing of sugar beets is more sophisticated than the simple home processing techniques that were used in the late 1800s. However, that traditional home processing procedure is the method that is described in this chapter.

Growing:
Sugar beet seeds should be planted in the early spring. The beets grow below ground like carrots. The sugar beet roots are harvested in the fall after the first hard frost. They contain between 14% to 21% sucrose sugar by weight. When harvested the beets should be knocked together to shake off most of the dirt that is still clinging to the beet roots. (Note: Regular beets only contain about 5% to 6% sucrose by weight so be sure to use the special sugar beets.)

Preparation:
Cut off the top of the beet with its leaves. (Note: The leaves contain protein, carbohydrates, and vitamin A and they may be eaten like normal beet greens, or they may be used as a livestock feed when combined with other types of feed.)
Carefully wash and scrub the beet to remove any remaining dirt particles.
Then cut the beet into pieces using any one of the following three methods:
1. Slice the beet into extremely thin slices, or
2. Slice and dice the beet into very small tiny cubes, or
3. Shred the beet using a vegetable shredder.

Cooking:
1. Transfer the cut beets to a large pot and add just barely enough water to completely cover the beets.
2. Cook the beets over medium heat, stirring frequently, until they are soft and tender. This takes about one-hour.
3. Use a thin clean towel and strain the water off the beets and save the *beet sugar water*. You may eat the cooked beets immediately or you may preserve the cooked beets for later consumption by canning or freezing. (Note: Commercial beet processors press or squeeze the beets at this point to extract as much of the sugar as possible from the beets. You may add this step if you wish or you may simply eat the beets.)
4. Simmer the *beet sugar water* over low to medium heat, stirring frequently, until it becomes a sweet thick dark *beet sugar syrup* similar to honey or molasses. Then turn off the heat.

Crystallization:
Although the beet sugar syrup will very slowly crystallize into sugar, the process takes a very long time. Therefore most families immediately begin using their beet sugar syrup as a sweetener instead of waiting for it to crystallize. The beet sugar syrup may be used in most recipes instead of the sugar (and some of the water) specified in the recipe.

If you want to wait a very long time for the syrup to crystallize then do the following:
1. Wait for the sweet dark *beet sugar syrup* to cool. Then transfer the beet sugar syrup to a storage container. The *beet sugar syrup* will slowly and gradually begin to crystallize over a period of many, many months the same way that honey slowly begins to crystallize.
2. As the sugar slowly and gradually crystallizes you should periodically remove it from the container and then break, crush, or pound it into small *beet sugar crystals*.

Beet Sugar Crystals:
Homemade *beet sugar* is chemically the same type of sugar as regular cane sugar and therefore it may be stored and used in the same manner as cane sugar. However, since homemade beet sugar is produced using a different extraction process it will have slightly different baking characteristics. The most noticeable baking difference is that it does not have the caramelization characteristic of commercially processed cane sugar.

Sugar Crystallization Footnote 1: The normal crystallization process can take a very, very long time and it is not unusual for a family to consume all their sweet dark *beet sugar syrup* before it has time to crystallize.

Sugar Crystallization Footnote 2: The normal crystallization process can be accelerated by cooking the *beet sugar syrup* down almost into sugar crystals.

Other Uses for the Beet Sugar Water and the Beet Sugar Syrup:

Alcoholic Beverage: The *beet sugar water* may be fermented to make a type of "rum" or a type of "vodka." These alcoholic drinks are very popular in Czechoslovakia and Germany.

Sweet Thick Beet Sugar Syrup: The sweet thick "honey like" *beet sugar syrup* may be spread on bread or pancakes and eaten. It may also be used as a substitute for honey in dessert recipes.

Chapter Six

Simple Bean Recipes

Dry Beans

Sorting and Rinsing Dry Beans: Look through your dry beans and remove any small foreign particles such as tiny sticks, stones, or other debris. Rinse the dry beans thoroughly and discard the rinse water.

Soaking or Hydrating: Do not soak lentils, split peas, black-eyed peas, or mung beans.
For each cup of dry beans add 2 or 3 cups of water. If fresh water is easily available then use three cups of water per cup of dry beans. However, if fresh water is not readily available then you may use two cups of water per cup of dry beans. The advantage of the extra water is that the extra water can more easily and quickly absorb the undesirable chemicals from the beans.
Soak the beans overnight (between 8 to 14 hours) in a cool place. Drain the beans and discard the soak water. The soak water will contain undesirable chemicals that have been leeched out of the beans. The soak water will also contain a small quantity of healthy nutrients but those nutrients will be mixed in with undesirable chemicals. Therefore the soak water should be discarded for health and safety reasons.

Cooking: If beans are not thoroughly cooked then they are more difficult to chew and digest, and they will generate more gas during the digestive process.

Toxin Neutralization: In order to neutralize any minor amount of toxins that may still be in the beans, bring the beans in the cook pot to a boil and boil for ten minutes. Then reduce the heat to a simmer.

Optional Seasonings During Cooking: Thinly sliced strips of meat (beef or ham or pork or bacon), or chopped onions, or chopped celery may be added while the beans are simmering. This will allow the beans to fully absorb these flavors while they are cooking.
Do not add salt or acids (tomatoes, catsup, wine, or vinegar) to the beans while they are cooking. These items slow down the cooking and softening process. Add salt and acids (tomatoes or catsup) after the beans are fully cooked.

Slow Cooking (recommended): Put a lid or cover on the cook pot. The slower the beans are cooked the easier it is for the human body to digest them. Slowly simmering the beans over very low heat for between 3 to 8 hours is ideal.

Fast Cooking (not recommended): The minimum cooking time for beans over medium heat is 60 to 90 minutes. Soybeans should be cooked for three hours.

Additional Water: To prevent scorching you may need to add water to the beans as they cook because some of the water will be absorbed into the beans and some of the water will evaporate due to the heat. Do not add cool water or cold water to the beans while they are cooking because the cool water shock will toughen the beans and they will require a longer cooking time and the beans will be a little harder to digest. Instead heat the extra water in a separate cook pot and then add the hot water to the bean pot.

Maximum Cooking Temperature: Do not cook beans at a temperature higher than 167 degrees Fahrenheit (or 75 degrees C).

Cooked Bean Test: When the bean is soft and it can be easily mashed with a fork using just a little pressure, then the bean is done.

Optional Seasonings After Cooking: After the beans are fully cooked then you may add salt, tomatoes, wine, or vinegar or any other acidic ingredient. Then simmer the beans over very low heat for a short period of time to give the beans a chance to absorb the new flavors.

Refried Beans

| 1 can pinto beans | 2 tbsp. oil | 1 tsp. onion powder |

Heat oil and add the onion powder. Add the cooked pinto beans. Mash the beans with the back of a wooden spoon or potato masher. Simmer for 6 minutes over low heat. May be eaten as a side dish or mixed half-and-half with ground meat as a filling for tacos or burritos or stuffed peppers.

Chapter Seven

Simple Potato Recipes

Potato Cakes

| Leftover mashed potatoes | Flour and oil (or lard) |

Form the leftover cooked mashed potatoes into flat small 4 inch circles about 3/8 inch thick. Coat each side with a thin layer of flour. Fry in a little oil in a pan over medium heat, turning once, until brown on both sides.

Hash Brown Potatoes

2 cups cooked diced potatoes	1 tsp. pepper
2 tsp. onion powder	1 tsp. salt

Heat a little oil or shortening in a large skillet. Spread the potatoes evenly over the bottom of the skillet and sprinkle the onion, pepper, and salt on top. Cook over low heat and press down on the potatoes several times with a flat spatula. When the bottom side is golden brown, cut the potatoes in half with the spatula and flip both halves over and brown the other side, pressing down with the spatula several times.

Potato Chips

Preparation: Peel raw potatoes and slice extremely thin. Soak in cold water for 1 hour. Then pat dry and try to remove as much water as possible.
Cook: Fry in oil preheated to 390°F. Remove and drain on paper towel. Sprinkle with salt. Allow to cool (optional).

Chapter Eight

Simple White Rice Recipes

1 cup **uncooked** dry rice = 3 cups **cooked** rice

Measure the white rice. Do **not** rinse the rice. Boil the rice in twice the volume of water with a pinch of salt. Trickle the white rice into the water so the water doesn't stop boiling. Cover the pot and let it simmer 15 to 18 minutes over very low heat until all the water is absorbed. Do not stir while simmering. Stirring causes the grains to stick together. Do not lift the lid until the rice is almost done or you will release essential steam and moisture. When done, remove the pot from the heat and fluff the rice with a fork. Cover and let stand another 5 minutes. The rice will continue to steam and absorb flavors.

Rice Substitutions

White rice can be substituted for bread crumbs in meatloaf, in meatball, and in poultry stuffing recipes. Rice can also be used to add body and texture to any soup.

Rice Flour

Uncooked white rice can be ground into a fine powder. It can then be used as a thickener or binder instead of flour. It is particularly useful for sauces. It can be cooked with milk and flavorings for a smooth dessert (see the Rice Sundae Dessert Recipe in the Dessert Chapter). Since rice does not contain gluten it can't be used to make a yeast bread loaf. However, it can be added to biscuits to improve their texture, and to cake, pancake, and pizza dough. It can be used in equal amounts with wheat flour or cornmeal. However, most people prefer a 1/4 to 1/3 ratio of white rice flour to wheat flour.

The Basic Burrito (or Stuffed Tortilla)

A little cooked white rice can be added to the other ingredients in a Burrito, such as refried beans and meat (ground or sliced).

Rice and Beans

The meal of choice for balanced nutrition and energy. Any type of beans may be used. Any ratio of white rice to beans may be used. However, most people prefer a ratio of half rice and half beans. The addition of some diced onion to the mixture is a flavor enhancement preferred by many people.

Feathered Rice (Serves Four)

| 1 cup **uncooked** white rice | 1 tsp. salt | 2.5 cups boiling water |

Unlike ordinary cooked white rice, this recipe causes the rice to puff up and become light and fluffy. Preheat oven to 400°F. Spread the **uncooked** white rice evenly on a shallow baking pan. Place in the oven and bake at 400°F, stirring occasionally, until the rice is a golden brown. Put the rice into a 1-quart casserole dish and then add the salt and the boiling water. Cover with a tight-fitting lid and bake at 400°F for 20 minutes. (Note: A pound of white rice may be browned and then stored in an airtight container until it is ready to be baked.)

Baked Rice (Serves Four)

1 cup **uncooked** white rice	2 tbsp. butter	1 tbsp. onion powder
2 cups water	2 chicken (or beef) bouillon cubes	

Preheat oven to 375°F. In a saucepan, melt the butter and add the onion powder and simmer over low heat for two minutes. Add the white rice and stir continually for 3 minutes until all the rice is coated. Add the water and bring to a boil. Add the bouillon cubes and allow them to dissolve and mix well. Pour into a 1-quart casserole, cover, and bake at 375°F for 30 minutes.
Optional: Dice a green pepper and add it with the bouillon cubes.
Optional: Add up to 1 cup of diced Spam when pouring into the casserole dish.

Mexican or Spanish Rice (Serves Four)

1 cup **uncooked** white rice	2 tbsp. oil	1 tsp. onion powder
1/4 cup diced tomatoes	2 cups chicken broth	1 tbsp. butter
1 tsp. garlic powder	1/8 cup diced green peppers	

Heat the oil and butter in a 2 quart pan over medium heat. When the butter is melted, add the white rice and simmer, stirring constantly, for about 3 minutes until lightly browned. Add the onion and garlic and continue to simmer and stir for 5 more minutes. Add the broth and bring to a boil without stirring. Reduce heat. Gently stir in the tomatoes and peppers. Cover and simmer until all the liquid is absorbed (about 15 to 18 minutes). When done, remove the pot from the heat and fluff the rice with a fork. Cover and let stand another 5 minutes. The rice will continue to steam and absorb flavors.

Indian Rice (Serves Four)

1 cup **uncooked** white rice	1/4 tsp. ground turmeric or rosemary	1/2 tsp. salt
2 cups water	1/2 tsp. ground cinnamon	1/4 tsp. pepper
1 tbsp. onion powder	2/3 cup raisins (optional)	

Heat 2 tbsp. water to boiling in a 2-quart saucepan over medium heat. Add the onion powder, cinnamon, salt, pepper, and turmeric (or rosemary) and stir. Add the remaining water and heat to boiling. Add the white rice and reduce heat. Cover and simmer for 15 to 20 minutes without stirring until all the liquid is absorbed. Fluff the rice with a fork and then stir in the raisins (optional), cover, and let stand 5 minutes.

Herb Flavored Rice (Serves Four)

1 cup **uncooked** white rice	1/4 tsp. salt	1 tbsp. butter
2.5 cups water	1/4 tsp. oregano	1 tbsp. onion powder
1/2 tsp. ground sage	1/4 tsp. thyme	

Melt the butter in 2.5-quart saucepan over medium heat. Add 2 tbsp. water and bring to a boil. Add the salt, onion, sage, oregano, thyme, and stir. Add the remaining water and heat to boiling. Add the white rice and reduce heat. Cover and simmer for 30 to 45 minutes without stirring until all the liquid is absorbed.

Chapter Eight: White Rice

Rice Pilaf (Serves Four)

1 cup **uncooked** white rice	3 tbsp. olive oil	1/2 tsp. salt
2 cups beef broth	1 tbsp. onion powder	1/4 tsp. pepper

Heat the oil and the onion powder in a saucepan. Add the white rice and simmer over low heat for 3 minutes. Add the salt, pepper, and beef broth. Cover saucepan and cook for 20 minutes (or transfer to a covered casserole and bake at 350°F for 1 hour).
Optional: Sauté 1 cup chopped mushrooms in 2 tbsp. butter and add with the broth.
Optional: Replace beef with chicken broth and add 1/2 tsp. tarragon.
Optional: Add 1 cup cooked diced beef or chicken with the broth.

Rice-A-Roni (Serves Four)

Follow the above recipe for Rice Pilaf but add 1 cup of Spaghetti noodles broken into small pieces one-inch or shorter. Brown the broken spaghetti in the oil with the onion powder at the beginning of the above Rice Pilaf recipe.

Stuffed Grape (or Cabbage) Leaves (Serves Six)

30 young grape leaves	1/2 cup oil	1 tbsp. dried mint
1 cup **uncooked** white rice	1/2 tbsp. onion powder	1 tbsp. parsley or dill or both
3 cups cooked ground meat	1 tbsp. garlic powder	1/2 tsp. salt and 1/4 tsp. pepper

Drop the leaves (about 4-inch diameters) in boiling water for 30 seconds and remove with a slotted spoon, drain, and set aside. Heat 4 tbsp. of oil in a saucepan and add the onion powder. Add the garlic, mint, parsley, salt, and pepper. Simmer for 5 minutes. Mix in the uncooked white rice and the cooked ground meat. Remove from heat. Place a leaf shiny side down and put 1 to 2 tbsp. of the mixture in the center of the leaf. Fold like an envelope and roll up but not too tightly. Put the rest of the oil in the bottom of a pot or Dutch oven and arrange the leaf rolls in rows and layers with the seam side down. Cover the rolls with water. Put a lid on the pot and simmer on low heat for 35 minutes.
Variation: Instead of grape leaves, use cabbage leaves, spinach leaves, etc.
Variation: Instead of ground meat, cover the leaf rolls with beef broth instead of water and simmer for 35 minutes.

Hamburger, Rice, and Scrambled Eggs (Serves Six)

1 pound hamburger	1 cup **uncooked** white rice	6 fresh eggs

Optional Items: Diced onion, diced tomatoes, diced sweet green peppers.
The hamburger, rice, and eggs can be cooked at the same time but in different skillets and pots.
Break the raw hamburger into very small pieces and fry in a skillet. Drain the grease off the hamburger.
In a separate cook pot prepare the white rice according to the instructions on page 13.
In a separate non-stick skillet scramble the six eggs according to the instructions on page 4.
When the hamburger, rice, and scrambled eggs are all done then mix them all together in a large serving bowl (or in the skillet that was used to cook the hamburger). Serve while still warm.
Variation: You may substitute wild game meat that has been finely ground for the hamburger.
Variation: Add the diced onion to the raw hamburger and cook both at the same time. When the hamburger is almost done, add the diced tomatoes and/or the diced sweet green peppers and stir and allow them to heat while the hamburger finishes cooking. Then mix thoroughly with the rice and eggs.

Chapter Eight: White Rice

Fried Rice (Leftover White Rice) (Serves One)

1/2 cup **cooked** white rice	2 tbsp. oil	1/2 tsp. salt
1/2 tsp. garlic powder	1 tbsp. soy sauce	1/4 tsp. pepper
1 tbsp. onion powder	1 tbsp. catsup	green onion (optional)

Heat the oil in a frying pan or wok. Add the garlic and onion powders and stir-fry for 30 seconds. Add the cooked white rice and stir-fry until coated with oil. Stir in the soy sauce and catsup. Add salt and pepper to taste. Heat for a few minutes until very hot. Serve immediately. If available, garnish with diced or shredded wild green onion.

Sweet Rice (Leftover White Rice) (Serves One)

1/2 cup **cooked** white rice	2 tbsp. butter
1 tbsp. sugar (granulated or brown)	1/2 tsp. cinnamon

Combine all and heat in the oven or in a microwave until warm. Serve as a sweet breakfast treat, or as an afternoon snack, or as a dessert.

Pot Luck Pie (Leftover White Rice) (Serves Six)

1 Pie Crust	Assorted leftover vegetables, **cooked** white rice, and/or cooked meat

Mix **any** combination of different, assorted leftovers together (at least 3 or 4 different items) and put them all inside a pie crust. Put a top on the pie and bake in a 350°F oven for 30 minutes. The pie is absolutely delicious. The flavor and versatility of this pot luck pie recipe is rarely appreciated until after it has been tried at least once.

Warm Rice and Tuna (Serves Four)

2 cups **cooked** white rice	3 tbsp. butter	1 tbsp. celery powder
5 oz. can tuna, drained	1 tbsp. onion powder	1 tbsp. parsley flakes

Melt the butter in a saucepan. Add the onion, celery, and parsley and simmer for 2 minutes. Add the tuna and the cooked white rice. Stir while heating thoroughly. Add salt and pepper as desired.
Variation: Substitute one cup of diced Spam for the tuna.

Chilled Rice and Tuna Salad (Serves Four)

2 cups **cooked** white rice	1 or 2 green onions, minced
5 oz. can tuna in oil	1 or 2 tomatoes, cut into small wedges
1 pickle, minced	1/2 cup mushrooms or olives (optional)

Mix all ingredients and serve cold.
Variation: Substitute one cup of diced Spam for the tuna.

Chilled Rice, Tuna, and Fruit Salad (Serves Four)

1.5 cups **cooked** white rice	5 oz. can tuna, drained	16 oz. can fruit cocktail, drained

Combine the cooked white rice and fruit cocktail. Mix well. Refrigerate for 1 hour to blend the flavors. Stir in the tuna and serve.
Variation: Substitute one cup of diced Spam for the tuna.

Chapter Nine

Meat Recipes

Chicken Fried Steak

Cut the meat (steak) into pieces about 6 inches long and less than 1 inch thick. Pound flour into the steaks using a meat tenderizer mallet. Pound in a much flour as you can until the steaks are saturated and quite thin. Sprinkle generously with salt and pepper. Heat a little shortening, fat, or oil in a large skillet over high heat. Cook the steaks very quickly, about 2 to 3 minutes on each side, until golden brown. Make gravy by mixing a little flour with the grease in the pan. Serve immediately.

Southern Fried Chicken

3/8 cup flour	1/8 tsp. pepper
3 tbsp. shortening, fat, or oil	1/2 tsp. salt

Wash and dry chicken. Mix ingredients in plastic zipper bag. Shake each piece of chicken inside the bag until well coated. Brown chicken quickly in fat, shortening, or oil. Reduce heat and cover skillet. Cook slowly. Only turn once.
Variation: Use 1/4 cup flour and 1/4 cup cornmeal. Apply a light coating to the chicken. Too much will make a dry, hard crust.

Northern Fried Chicken

Prepare as above. Add 1/2 cup water before covering skillet. Simmer slowly for 30 minutes until tender. Remove lid and let chicken fry slowly until done.

Chicken Parts

Simmer gizzard and heart in water until almost tender before frying. Liver requires only a few minutes of cooking. Thick pieces of chicken take longer to cook than the smaller, thin pieces.

Chicken and Dumplings

2 cans of chicken	1/2 tsp. salt	1 cup butter
2 cans chicken broth	1/2 tsp. pepper	Enough biscuit dough for 12 biscuits

Put everything **except** the biscuit dough in a pot and bring to a boil. Add the biscuit dough to the pot by spoonfuls and then immediately turn down the heat to a simmer. Continue to simmer gently until the biscuit dough is done (taste test).

Chicken Broth

2 pounds chicken scraps (back, neck, wings, etc.)	10 chicken feet
1 tbsp. celery or sweet herbs	2 quarts cold water
1 tsp. salt and 2 peppercorns	1 tbsp. onion powder

Scald chicken feet, skin and remove nails. Clean chicken and remove fat. Cut chicken into small pieces and crack the bones. Cover chicken with cold water and add a pinch of salt. Let stand 20 minutes. Drain well and removed any blood clots and any remaining fat. Add all the above ingredients and simmer 3 hours. Strain through a clean cloth. Cool quickly and skim fat from surface. Cool again. Ladle broth into plastic containers (do **not** pour). Discard the cloudy broth in the bottom of the bowl. Reheat when ready to serve.

Beef Broth

Use beef soup bones and some lean, thin, diced pieces of beef. Let bones and beef stand in cold water one hour and then follow the recipe for "Chicken Broth" except simmer 6 hours.

Shish Kabobs (Kebabs)

Long Metal Skewers	Green Pepper, Mushrooms
Meat (Beef, Vienna Sausage, Spam)	Potatoes, Tomatoes, Onion

Preparation: Boil raw potatoes. Cook raw beef. (If using canned beef or canned potatoes then they are already pre-cooked.) Alternate available items on skewer, so each item touches the ones beside it.
Cook: Heat over a campfire until tasty.

Roast Beef Hash

16 oz. can roast beef	1 tbsp. onion powder
32 oz. can potatoes	1 tbsp. olive oil

Preparation: Drain potatoes well. Grind the meat, potatoes, and onion together using a meat grinder.
Cook: Heat oil in large frying pan. Slide hash into pan without splattering. Spread hash over bottom of pan. Stir or turn with spatula until well heated. Hash makes a satisfying one-dish meal. May be served with salsa or catsup or with scrambled eggs.
Variation: Use 8 oz. of roast beef and 8 oz. of ham.
Variation: Add can of mushrooms, diced.

Beans and Wieners

1 can Pork & Beans	1 can Vienna Sausage

Slice each Vienna Sausage into 6 or 7 pieces. Mix with beans and heat in cook pot until ready to eat.
Optional: Add 1/8 cup diced onions and/or 1 tbsp. catsup.

Pigs in a Blanket

1 can Vienna Sausage	1 tsp. baking powder	1/2 cup lard
2 cups wheat flour	1 tsp. salt	warm water

Preparation: Mix all (except sausage) to make a smooth dough. Roll dough into large flat rectangle and cut into 3 inch squares. Wrap each square around a Vienna Sausage. (Optional: Pinch ends together.)
Cook: Preheat oven to 350°F. Place the wrapped sausages on a greased baking pan so they don't touch each other. Cover pan and bake for 20 minutes or until lightly browned.

Tuna Casserole

5 oz. can tuna	14 oz. box macaroni and cheese mix
3 tbsp. instant dry milk	1/2 cup water

Preparation: Mix macaroni and cheese according to the box directions, but also add the tuna, and use the instant milk and water in place of the fresh milk. (Or use fresh milk, if available.)
Cook: Bake at 350°F for 20 minutes.

Chapter Nine: Meat

Salmon (or Mackerel) Patties

15 oz. can salmon (or mackerel)	1/2 cup cornmeal
salt and pepper	1 egg (optional)

Preparation: Mix everything in a large bowl. Form patties 1/4 inch thick and 4 inches in diameter.
Cook: Fry in some oil or butter in a hot skillet until golden brown on both sides.

Spaghetti with Meat Balls

16 oz. spaghetti noodles	4 quarts water
26 oz. spaghetti sauce	1/3 cup uncooked oatmeal (optional)
16 oz. ground meat	2 tsp. Worcestershire sauce (optional)

Variation: Thin or angel hair spaghetti noodles will cook faster than regular noodles.
Variation: The ground meat may be hamburger or almost any type of ground wild game meat.
Meatballs: Preheat oven to 350ºF. In a large bowl combine the ground meat, the uncooked oatmeal, and the Worcestershire sauce. Mix until the ingredients are well blended. Form into balls about the size of a walnut and place the meatballs on a baking sheet or cookie sheet. Place the baking sheet on the center shelf of a 350ºF oven and bake the meatballs for twenty minutes. While the meatballs are cooking you can heat the spaghetti sauce and cook the spaghetti noodles. When the meatballs are done, remove them from the baking sheet using a spatula or some tongs and add them to the skillet with the hot spaghetti sauce.
Spaghetti Sauce: You may heat some canned spaghetti sauce or you can make your own homemade sauce using the recipe on page 7. If you make you own spaghetti sauce then it will take at least one hour and it should be made before you begin cooking the meatballs or the noodles.
Spaghetti Noodles: You may break a small handful of dry spaghetti noodles into halves or thirds before cooking them. My family, and especially my grandchildren, prefer the dry noodles to be broken into three equal lengths before cooking them because this makes the cooked noodles much easier to eat and enjoy at the dining table. Follow the box instructions and boil the noodles in the correct amount of water for the correct amount of time based on the type of noodles you are using (regular, thin, or angel hair). Breaking the noodles into halves or thirds will not change the total boiling time for the noodles.
Spaghetti, Sauce, and Meatballs: You may combine the noodles, sauce, and meatballs together in one large skillet and then transfer individual servings to each person's plate. However, instead of combining the noodles and sauce together in one skillet you may allow each person to fill his or her own plate with the amount of noodles desired, and then add the amount of meat sauce and meatballs desired on top of or beside his or her noodles. This allows each person the option to prepare his or her meal they way he or she prefers.

Chili with Beans (or Chili Con Carne)

16 oz. ground meat	1/4 cup diced onion	1.5 cups diced tomatoes (or canned tomatoes)		
15 oz. canned beans	1 tsp. granulated sugar	1 tbsp. chili powder	1 tsp. salt	1 tsp. pepper

Variation: Either kidney beans or pinto beans may be used depending on your taste preferences. If you wish to use dry beans instead of canned beans then follow the dry bean cooking recipe on page 11.
Variation: The ground meat may be hamburger or almost any type of ground wild game meat.
Cook: Cook the ground meat with the diced onion in a large skillet until well done. (Drain and discard the grease if you wish.) Add the other ingredients, put a cover on the skillet, and simmer over very low heat for one hour or longer, stirring occasionally. A longer cooking time creates a thicker chili.
Optional: Serve with crackers. You may add diced onions or shredded cheese on top of the chili.

Chapter Nine: Meat

Chapter Ten

Introduction to all the Bread Recipes

Yeast Bread Recipes

Most bread recipes require yeast and eggs. Yeast causes the bread to rise and become light. Eggs add protein, color, and bulk to the bread. Under hardship conditions you may have limited amounts of both yeast and fresh eggs.

The good news is that yeast multiplies and a little yeast can last a very, very, long time if you follow the simple directions below.

The bad news is that eggs don't multiply. Once they have been used, they are gone. And if you only have a few eggs during hard times, then you may wish to use them for something other than baking.

If you have store-bought eggs then don't try to hatch them because they were laid by hens on an egg farm without roosters. Hens can lay eggs without a rooster but the eggs won't be fertile without a rooster.

Most of the following bread recipes do require yeast but they no **not** require eggs. However, some of the recipes do permit the use of an optional egg.

Yeast Preparation

Freeze store bought yeast until it is needed. Before using the yeast remove it from the freezer and allow it to warm up to room temperature. Then stir a little crumbled yeast into some warm water (105°F to 115°F). Test the water on your wrist. It should feel warm but not hot. If the water is too hot it will kill the yeast. If the water is too cold it will slow down the process. Adding a little sugar to the water will speed up the process. Adding salt or fat will slow it down. Good yeast will become foamy and creamy after about 10 to 12 minutes.

All Yeast Breads

Don't waste your package yeast. After you have added yeast to some bread dough, pinch off one handful of the bread dough **after the first rise** and save it in an airtight container in a cool dark place. The next day mix the old dough into a new batch of dough. The yeast will multiply and spread throughout the new batch. After the first rise, pinch off a handful of dough and save it. Continue this process each time you make yeast bread and you will be able to make bread for a very long time from that one original package of yeast.

Optional Crust Variations for All Breads

Just before putting the bread dough into the oven, use a pastry brush to carefully and very gently paint the top of the dough.

1. Cold water brushed or sprayed on the bread dough will yield a crisp, chewy crust.
2. Oil or melted butter will yield a soft crust.
3. 1 tbsp. honey with 2 tbsp. water yields a sweet, glossy finish.
4. 1 tbsp. lemon juice with 2 tbsp. sugar gives a fruity, sweet flavor.
5. 1 egg white beaten with 1 tbsp. water gives a shiny, crisp crust.
6. 1 egg white beaten with 1 tbsp. milk gives a shiny, softer crust.
7. 1 whole egg with 2 tbsp. water gives a shiny, rich, dark crust.

Liquid Substitutions

Water: Yields a chewy texture with more of the original flour flavor.

Milk: Bread will rise higher and have a finer texture and it will keep longer. Heat fresh milk until it almost boils to kill the enzymes that interfere with the yeast action in the bread. Do not heat canned milk or instant milk. Milk also adds nutritional value to the finished bread.

Buttermilk: Bread will be more tender. Heat the buttermilk until it almost boils. Do not use too much or it will make the bread too tender and it will fall apart.

Potato Water: The water left over after boiling potatoes. It will cause the bread to rise higher and it will add a coarser texture and moistness. Do not substitute more than 1/2 potato water for the normal water required in the recipe.

Oils or Butter: Adds tenderness and improves the elasticity of the bread. Increases bulk and helps the bread to brown more evenly. However, too much oil will make the bread crumbly. Use a maximum of 1 tbsp. oil or shortening or butter per 1 cup of flour.

Wheat Berry Sprouting Water: Adds nutrition, texture, and flavor enhancement to the bread.

Miscellaneous Optional Ingredients

Eggs: Adds protein, color, and bulk. Eggs help to extend the shelf life of the bread. For each egg used, deduct 1/4 cup of the other liquid in the recipe. Use no more than 2 eggs per loaf of bread.

Honey: Maximum of 1 tbsp. per 1 cup of flour. Adds flavor and moistness and helps to feed the yeast and increases the shelf life of the bread.

Salt: Maximum of 1/2 tsp. per 1 cup of flour. Controls the yeast process. Improves flavor and increases the shelf life of the bread. A bread made with no salt will taste flat. Do **not** add the salt to the yeast water or it will inhibit the initial yeast process.

Wheat Flour and Wheat Berries

Wheat Flour: The recipes in this cookbook normally specify wheat flour.

Wheat Berries: If you have wheat berries then you will need to grind them into a wheat flour that is of a consistency that your family prefers.

Chapter Eleven

Yeast Bread Recipes

100% Whole Wheat Loaf Bread (Recipe One)
(Must be eaten in two days or slice it and freeze it)

3 cups wheat flour	2 tbsp. oil	2 tbsp. honey	1 tsp. salt
1/2 pkg. yeast (1/2 tbsp.)	1 cup warm water	1/3 cup instant nonfat dry milk	

Preparation: Dissolve yeast in warm water and let stand 12 minutes. Add oil, honey, dry milk, salt, and enough wheat flour to make a stiff dough. Allow to rest under an inverted bowl for 10 minutes. Then knead for 10 minutes. Place in greased bowl, cover, and let rise until double in bulk or about 90 minutes. Punch down and form into ball. Cover and let rest for 10 minutes. Shape into a loaf and place in greased loaf pan. Cover and let rise until double in bulk, about 45 to 60 minutes.
Cook: Bake at 375°F for 40 minutes. Brush hot loaf with milk.

100% Whole Wheat Loaf Bread (Recipe Two)
(Must be eaten in two days or slice it and freeze it)

2.25 cups wheat flour	1 tbsp. melted butter	2.5 tbsp. honey	1 tsp. salt
1/2 pkg. yeast (1/2 tbsp.)	3/4 cup warm water	1 tbsp. instant nonfat dry milk	

Follow the above Recipe One preparation and cooking instructions but substitute the butter for the oil.

100% Whole Wheat French Bread

3 cups wheat flour	3/4 cup cold water	1.5 tsp. salt
1/2 pkg. yeast (1/2 tbsp.)	1/4 cup warm water	

Preparation: Dissolve yeast in warm water for 12 minutes. Sift wheat flour and salt together. Add yeast and cold water. Knead for 20 minutes and add at least 1/2 cup more cold water by wetting your hands as your knead. Dough should be soft and silky. Cover and let rise in cool place for 3 hours. Punch down gently with wet hands being careful not to tear dough. Cover and let rise again in a cool place for 2 hours. Punch down and form into a ball. Cover and let rest while you dust a baking sheet with corn meal. Shape dough into a long slim loaf. Place on baking sheet. Let rise uncovered for 1 hour. Cut slashes in top of loaf.
Cook: Spray loaf with warm water. Quickly place in 450°F oven. Place shallow pan with boiling water on oven rack below bread. After 10 minutes reduce the heat to 350°F. Bake another 25 to 30 minutes.
Optional: Add 2 tbsp. oil, or 1.5 tbsp. sugar, or both to the above recipe with the flour and salt.

Sandwich Buns (12 Buns)

3 cups wheat flour	2.5 tbsp. oil	1/2 cup sugar	1/2 tsp. salt
1/2 pkg. yeast (1/2 tbsp.)	1 cup warm water	2.5 tbsp. instant nonfat dry milk	

Preparation: Dissolve yeast in warm water and let stand 12 minutes. Then add sugar, salt, oil, dry milk, and 3/4 cup flour. Beat vigorously by hand. Stir in additional flour to make a stiff dough. Knead on a floured board until smooth and elastic (10 minutes). Place in greased bowl, cover, and let rise in warm place for 45 minutes. Punch dough down. Let rise again about 20 minuets. Divide dough and form into 12 balls. Place on greased baking sheet 2 inches apart. Let rest for 5 minutes. Press down with palm to flatten. Cover and let rise in warm place for 1 hour.
Cook: Bake at 375°F for 15 to 20 minutes. Remove from baking sheet and let cool on wire racks.

Hard Rolls (9 Rolls)

2.25 cups wheat flour	1 tsp. sugar	1/2 tsp. salt
1/2 pkg. yeast (1/2 tbsp.)	1 cup warm water	2 tbsp. cornmeal

Preparation: Dissolve yeast in warm water and let stand for 12 minutes. Add sugar and salt. Stir well. Add 1.5 cups flour. Mix well. Cover and let rise for 20 minutes. Add the remaining flour and mix well. Knead for 5 minutes on a floured board. Cover and let rise 1 hour. Punch down and let rise again. Shape into 9 rolls. Place on lightly oiled baking sheet. Sprinkle with cornmeal. Slash tops with knife. Cover and let rise until doubled.
Cook: Bake at 400ºF on top oven rack with a pan of hot water on bottom oven rack for 20 to 25 minutes until golden brown.

Wheat Rolls (12 Rolls)

2 cups flour	1/8 cup sugar	1/4 tsp. salt
1/2 pkg. yeast (1/2 tbsp.)	1/4 cup warm water	1/4 cup warm milk

Preparation: Dissolve yeast in warm water and let stand 12 minutes. Stir in the warm milk, sugar, salt, and 1 cup of the flour. Mix until smooth. Cover the batter with a handful of flour and let rise in a warm place for about 2 hours or until the top has cracked. Add enough of the remaining flour to make a smooth dough and knead it for about 10 minutes. Cover and let rise 20 minutes. Shape into rolls and place on a baking sheet.
Cook: Bake at 400°F for about 15 to 20 minutes.

Whole Wheat Crescent Rolls (16 Rolls)

2.5 cups wheat flour	1 tbsp. brown sugar	1.5 tbsp. oil	1 tsp. salt
1/2 pkg. yeast (1/2 tbsp.)	7/8 cup warm water	2 tbsp. honey	3 tbsp. butter

Preparation: Dissolve yeast in warm water and let stand 12 minutes. Add brown sugar, oil, honey, salt, and 3/4 cup wheat flour. Mix well. Stir in enough of the remaining flour to make a stiff dough. Knead on a lightly floured surface for 10 minutes. Place in a greased bowl, cover, and let rise 90 minutes. Divide dough in half and shape into 2 balls. Cover and let rest 10 minutes. Roll each ball into an 8-inch to 10-inch circle. Spread with 1/3 of the butter. Cut each circle into 8 wedges. To make crescents, roll wide end of wedge toward point. Place on greased baking sheet. Cover and let rise 30 minutes.
Cook: Bake at 375°F for 12 to 15 minutes. Brush with milk or butter while still warm.

English Muffins (10 Muffins)

2 cups wheat flour	1/4 cup milk	1 tbsp. cornmeal	1/2 tsp. salt
1/2 pkg. yeast (1/2 tbsp.)	2 tbsp. warm water	1.5 tbsp. soft butter	1 tsp. sugar

Preparation: Dissolve yeast in 2 tbsp. warm water and let stand 12 minutes. In another bowl, combine milk, sugar and salt with one cup hot water. Add the yeast solution. Stir in 1 cup of flour. Cover bowl with a towel and let rise 90 minutes in a warm place. Stir in butter and remaining flour. Roll dough to 3/4 inch thickness. Cut 2.5 inch circles from dough and place on a piece of wax paper sprinkled with cornmeal. Sprinkle tops with more cornmeal. Let rise again.
Cook: Cook on a griddle, turning once.

Chapter Eleven: Yeast Breads

English Muffin Loaf

3 cups wheat flour	1/3 cup instant dry milk	2 tbsp. cornmeal	1 tsp. salt
1/2 pkg. yeast (1/2 tbsp.)	1.25 cups warm water	1/8 tsp. baking soda	1/2 tbsp. sugar

Preparation: Combine yeast, 1.5 cups flour, dry milk, sugar, salt, and baking soda. Mix well. Add the warm water. Beat well. Add remaining flour. Grease an 8-inch x 4-inch loaf pan. Sprinkle with cornmeal. Spoon the batter into the pan. Sprinkle top of loaf with cornmeal. Cover. Let rest 45 minutes.
Cook: Bake at 400°F for 25 minutes.

Pita Bread (2 Pieces)

2 cups wheat flour	1 tsp. sugar	1/2 tsp. salt
1 tsp. yeast	2 tbsp. warm water	2/3 cup warm water

Preparation: Dissolve yeast in 2 tbsp. warm water and let stand 12 minutes. Mix flour, sugar, and salt with 2/3 cup warm water. Add the yeast solution. Knead for 10 minutes. Put in greased bowl, cover, let rise for one-hour. Punch down, knead, reshape. Cover and let rise for 30 minutes. Divide into 2 parts. Roll each into an 8-inch diameter round. Place on greased cookie sheet.
Cook: Bake at 450°F for 5 minutes.

Bread on the Grill

2 cups wheat flour	1/2 tsp. sugar	1 tbsp. olive oil	1/2 tsp. salt
1/2 pkg. yeast (1/2 tbsp.)	3/4 cup warm water	2 tbsp. cornmeal	

Preparation: Dissolve yeast in warm water and let stand 12 minutes. Then add sugar, salt, oil, and flour. Beat vigorously by hand. Knead on a floured board until smooth and elastic (10 minutes). Place in greased bowl, cover, and let rise in warm place for 90 minutes. On a floured surface roll out half the dough into a 10-inch round circle. Rub both sides with cornmeal.
Cook: Brush grill rack with oil and fry 5 minutes on each side.

Pizza (One 14-inch Pizza)

1.75 cups flour	2 tsp. + 1 tbsp. olive oil	2/3 tsp. salt
1 tsp. yeast	2/3 cup warm water	1 tsp. sugar
1.5 cups tomato sauce or pizza sauce	1 cup grated mozzarella cheese	1 tsp. oregano

Pizza Sauce: You may use canned tomato sauce, or pizza sauce, or spaghetti sauce. Or you can make your own homemade pizza sauce using the recipe on page 8. If you make you own pizza sauce then it will take at least one hour and you could make it while your pizza dough is rising for two hours.
Pizza Dough: Dissolve yeast and sugar in 2/3 cup warm water. Let stand for 12 minutes. Add 1 cup flour, 2 tsp. oil, and salt and mix well. Continue to add flour to make a soft dough. Knead the dough on a floured board for 7 minutes until it is smooth and elastic. Put dough in an oiled bowl, cover with a cloth, and allow to rise in a warm place for 2 hours. Punch it down and let it rest 5 minutes. Roll the dough into a 14-inch circle using a rolling pin (or pat and stretch with your hands). Place on pizza pan (or cookie sheet) and prick all over with a fork. Cover with a cloth and let rest for 20 minutes.
Cook: Bake in 425°F oven for 3 minutes. Remove from oven. Spread tomato sauce or pizza sauce (or spaghetti sauce) evenly over crust. Sprinkle grated cheese and oregano evenly over sauce. (Optional: Add fully cooked meat, mushrooms, or vegetables as desired.) Drizzle 1 tbsp. olive oil over everything. Bake at 400°F for another 14 to 16 minutes until underside of crust is golden brown.

Chapter Eleven: Yeast Breads

Chapter Twelve

Bread Recipes without Yeast and without Eggs

Yeast causes the bread to rise and become light. Eggs add protein, color, and bulk to the bread. Eggs also increase the shelf life of the bread. Therefore most bread recipes require both yeast and eggs. It is relatively difficult to find good bread recipes that don't require yeast and/or eggs. And if you just omit the yeast or eggs from the original recipe then you normally end up with a culinary disaster that your family will not eat. To produce good bread without yeast or eggs, the recipe needs to be modified and other ingredients added to give the bread flavor and texture.

The following recipes don't require yeast or eggs. The reason is simple. Sometimes you will be completely out of yeast and fresh eggs but your family will still need to eat. You may have the other necessary ingredients to make bread but you don't have any yeast or fresh eggs. And a quick trip to the local store may not be an option. In a situation such at this, the following recipes can be used to produce delightful results to satisfy your family's desire for bread.

Pancakes (No Eggs)

2 cups flour	2 tbsp. baking powder	1/2 tsp. salt
1 cup milk	1 tbsp. vinegar	1 tbsp. honey

Mix all ingredients together well and then fry the pancakes on medium heat in a skillet. When the bubbles almost stop coming to the top then turn the pancakes once.

Flour Tortillas (14 six-inch Tortillas)

2 cups flour	1/2 to 1 tsp. salt	1/2 tsp. granulated sugar (optional)
1 tbsp. shortening	1/2 to 3/4 cup water	1/2 tbsp. baking powder (optional)

Preparation: Sift flour and salt together. (If desired, add optional sugar and/or baking powder.) Add shortening and mix well. Slowly add just enough water to form a soft dough. Cover and let stand for 30 minutes. Make about 14 two-inch balls. Press (or roll) each ball into a flat six-inch circle.
Cook: Fry over medium heat on ungreased flat griddle until golden brown on both sides (about 1.5 to 2 minutes per side).

Baking Powder Biscuits

2 cups wheat flour	1 tbsp. baking powder	1 tsp. salt
6 tbsp. butter or lard	1 cup milk or cream	1 tbsp. sugar (optional)

Preparation: Combine all dry ingredients and mix well. Blend in the warm butter. Slowly add the milk to the mixture until the dough holds together. Knead well and mold into small biscuits with your hands. Put on ungreased baking sheet.
Cook: Bake at 425°F for 15 to 20 minutes until lightly browned. Yields a sweet biscuit that will keep for days in a dry place.

Camp Biscuits or Biscuit Twists

1/2 cup flour	1/4 tsp. baking powder	1/4 tsp. salt
2 tbsp. oil or melted shortening or melted lard		warm water

Preparation: Mix flour, baking powder, and salt. Mix in oil or shortening. Add just enough warm water to make a stiff dough.
Camp Biscuits Cook: Drop by spoonfuls onto greased tin. Bake at 425°F until brown.
Biscuit Twists Cook: Mold dough into a ribbon about two-inches wide and thick as your little finger. Twist around a clean stick in a spiral fashion, and bake over hot coals near a campfire until done (similar to a roasted marshmallow).

Salt-Rising Bread (Recipe One)

3 cups wheat flour	1/2 cup milk	2 tbsp. brown sugar	1/2 tsp. salt
3.5 tbsp. cornmeal	1 cup lukewarm water	1.5 tbsp. oil or melted shortening	

Preparation: Bring milk almost to a boil. Remove from heat. Add the cornmeal, 1/2 tbsp. brown sugar, and salt. Put in a covered jar and place in a dish of hot water as hot as the hand can bear. Keep in a warm place overnight. By morning the mixture should show fermentation and gas can be heard to escape.
Then add 1 cup sifted wheat flour, 1.5 tbsp. oil, 1.5 tbsp. brown sugar, and 1 cup lukewarm water. Beat mixture thoroughly. Place in a dish of warm water again and let rise until light and full of bubbles. Then add 2 cups sifted wheat flour or enough to make a stiff dough. Knead for 10 or 15 minutes. Place into greased loaf pan and let rise again.
Cook: Bake 15 minutes at 425°F, then lower temperature to 375°F and bake about 30 minutes longer.

Salt-Rising Bread (Recipe Two)

8 cups wheat flour	2 cups milk	2 tsp. granulated sugar	1/2 tsp. salt
2 cups cornmeal	1 cup warm water	2 tbsp. oil or melted shortening	1/2 tsp. baking soda

Preparation: Bring milk almost to a boil. Remove from heat. Add the cornmeal, sugar, and salt. Stir until smooth. Cover with a towel and keep in a warm place overnight. In the morning, add one cup warm water, the baking soda, and 2.5 cups flour. Place the bowl in a pan of warm water and cover. Wait between 2 to 6 hours until the mixture starts to foam. As the original water cools, transfer the bowl to a new pan of warm water. Keep transferring the bowl to a new pan of warm water as the old water cools down. If the odor becomes very sour during this fermentation process then you will end up with a very sweet bread. After the batter has risen, add the oil and more flour until you have a stiff dough. Knead for 10 or 15 minutes. Shape into two loaves and place into two greased loaf pans and let rise again.
Cook: Bake about one hour at 350°F or until lightly brown.

Irish Soda Bread

2 cups wheat flour	1 tsp. baking soda	1/2 tsp. salt
1 tbsp. butter	3/4 cup buttermilk	1/2 tsp. cream of tartar

Substitution: 2 tsp. baking powder can be used to replace both the baking soda and the cream of tartar.
Preparation: Mix flour, baking soda, tartar, and salt in a bowl. Mix in the butter. Pour in the buttermilk and mix quickly and lightly to a soft dough. Put on a floured baking sheet. Shape into a round loaf (do **not** knead the dough). Cut an "X" one-half inch deep across the entire top of the loaf with a sharp knife. Sprinkle lightly with flour.
Cook: Bake in preheated 450°F oven 10 minutes. Then reduce to 400°F and bake another 10 minutes. Cool on a wire rack.

Sausage and Cheese Biscuits (makes 15 biscuits)

1/2 pound mild sausage (1 cup)	1 cup shredded cheddar cheese
1.5 cup Bisquick mix (page 5)	1/2 cup water

Preparation: Combine the Bisquick and the water and stir into a thick biscuit dough. Add the shredded cheese and stir until the cheese is well blended throughout the dough.
Cook: Break the sausage into very small pieces and fry in a skillet over medium heat until done. Add the cooked crumbled sausage, without the grease, to the Bisquick and cheese dough and stir thoroughly. Evenly distribute the sausage throughout the dough. Very lightly grease a cookie sheet. Use a spoon to drop large spoonfuls of the mixture onto the cookie sheet about 1.5 inches apart. You should create about 15 biscuit piles on the cookie sheet.
Bake: Preheat oven to 400°F. Place the cookie sheet of biscuits on the middle shelf in the oven. Bake at 400°F for twelve minutes. Remove from the oven and immediately use a plastic spatula to flip the biscuits upside down on the cookie sheet to keep the bottom of the biscuits from overcooking on the cookie sheet as the cookie sheet cools down. Allow the biscuits to cool for about two minutes but serve while they are still hot.

Choctaw Indian Fry Bread (Requires no sugar) (14 Pieces)
or Navaho Indian Fry Bread (Add 1 tsp. sugar to the following recipe)
or Indian Tortillas or Indian Fried Scones

2.25 cups wheat flour	1 tsp. salt	2 tsp. baking powder or soda
1/4 cup milk	3/4 cup water	2 tbsp. shortening (optional)

Preparation: Sift flour, salt, and baking powder into a bowl (with the optional 1 tsp. sugar). Stir in the water and milk (and the optional shortening). Knead with hands. Divide into about 12 balls with each ball about 1.5 inches in diameter. Cover and let rest for 20 minutes. Press each ball into a flat donut with a hole in the center. Use your thumb to start the hole and keep your thumb in the hole as you pat the ball into a flat circle against a flat surface.
Cook: Fry in 1 or 2 inches of hot oil (390°F) about 1 minute on each side or until puffed and golden brown. Drain on paper towel. Serve with honey.
Variation - Indian Tortillas: Use above Fry Bread Recipe but press the dough very thin.
Variation - Indian Fried Scones: Omit the milk. Increase water to 1 cup. Add 1 tbsp. sugar. Shape as scones and fry until golden brown. Serve with butter, honey, or jam.
Variation - Cornmeal Option: Add 1/3 cup cornmeal to the above recipe and increase the water to a total of 1 cup (instead of 3/4 cup).

Chapter Thirteen

Sourdough Bread Recipes
(No Eggs Required)

Sourdough Starter using a Fresh Potato

1 medium potato	1 pkg. yeast	4 cups water
2 cups + 2 tbsp. flour	2 tbsp. granulated sugar	

Peel medium potato, cut into cubes and boil cubed potato in about 3 cups water. Let stand in liquid until cool. Drain and reserve the potato water. Mash the potato and set aside 1/4 cup.
In a large bowl or crock, mix flour, sugar, and yeast.
In a saucepan, combine 1 cup potato water and 1 cup water. Warm to about 100 degrees. Pour over flour mix and add the 1/4 cup mashed potato, mixing well. Cover with waxed paper and then with foil. Crimp foil around edges, but not too tightly -- the starter has to breathe. Set aside at warm room temperature for 2 days. Uncover and stir in 2 tablespoons flour. Cover it back up and let sit 1 more day before using.
To feed: Every 2 or 3 days, stir in 2 tablespoons to 1/2 cup flour (depending on how often you use it). When you add the flour also add a pinch of sugar and just enough warm water to keep it similar to a thick pancake batter. You may refrigerate it to make it go dormant. When you need it again then bring to room temperature and feed as before.

Sourdough Starter using Instant Potatoes

6 tbsp. instant mashed potato flakes	1 pkg. rapid rise yeast
2/3 cup granulated sugar	2 cups warm water

Mix all ingredients in a glass jar and cover loosely with foil. The yeast will feed on the potato flakes and sugar, and the starter will give off gas as the yeast breeds. If the container is tightly sealed then the yeast will die off. Keep at room temperature for 24 hours then refrigerate. The starter must be feed at least every 10 days with 1 cup warm water, 1/3 cup sugar, and 3 tablespoons instant mashed potato flakes. You can freeze the starter in a plastic container until you are ready to bake.

Sourdough Starter using Honey

2 cups flour	1 pkg. yeast
2 tbsp. honey	2 cups warm water

Mix water, yeast, and honey. Stir to dissolve the yeast. Let stand 10 minutes. Stir in the flour and make a smooth dough. Cover and let stand at room temperature for two days, stirring twice a day. If a sour smelling liquid appears on the top then pour it off. Starter may be stored in a glass jar in the refrigerator until it is needed.

Sourdough Starter Water Base

| 2 cups flour | 1 pkg. dry yeast | 2 cups warm water |

Make this starter only when you have forgotten to save a starter. Combine ingredients and mix well. Place in warm place or closed cupboard overnight. In morning put 1/2 of the starter in a pint jar with a tight lid and store in refrigerator or cool place for future use. The remaining batter can be used for pancakes, waffles, bread, cake, etc. To use starter again place in mixing bowl. Add 2 cups water (or milk, if available) and 2 cups flour and starter. Beat well and set in warm place to develop over night. In the morning remove 1/2 of sponge for whatever you need it for and then put the rest back into a jar and refrigerate.

Sourdough Starter Buttermilk Base

| 1 cup flour | 1 cup buttermilk |

Mix flour and buttermilk and let stand 48 hours until fermented.
Then follow the above recipe for water base starter.

Sourdough Starter Milk Base

| 2 cups flour | 2 cups milk |

Put 2 cups of milk in a quart jar or pot. Cover with a double thickness of cheesecloth and secure with a rubber band. Let it stand at room temperature for 24 hours. Add the flour and mix well. Replace the cheesecloth and let it stand for 12 hours, preferably outdoors in a protected place. Bring indoors and keep in a warm place until the mixture is very bubbly. Put the mixture into a container that allows for adequate expansion (2 quarts). Keep covered in the refrigerator. When some of the starter is used, it should be replaced with equal amounts of milk and flour. The mixture should be used and replenished at least once per week. If you do not bake that often then pour out and discard half of the starter and replenish it with milk and flour once a week.

Variation: Water can be substituted for the milk, and the first 24 hours of the above process can be eliminated. However, the milk gives the starter a unique desirable flavor.

Sourdough Loaf Bread

| 1 cup sourdough starter | 1 tbsp. oil | 1 tsp. salt |
| 3 cups flour | 2/3 cups warm water | 1 pkg. yeast (optional) |

Preparation: If available, dissolve yeast in water in a large mixing bowl and let stand 10 minutes. Add the oil and the sourdough starter and mix well. Add the salt and 2 cups of flour. Beat until smooth. Gradually add 1 more cup of flour and continue mixing. Cover and let the dough rise until double in bulk (about 2 hours with yeast or about 6 hours without yeast). Then knead the dough on a floured board for 5 minutes. As necessary, add 1 tbsp. of flour until the dough is smooth and satiny. Place the dough in a greased bowl. Then rotate the dough inside the bowl so the top of the dough is also greased. Cover and let rise for 30 minutes. Punch down and knead for 2 minutes. Cover and let rise for 10 minutes. Grease two 9-inch loaf pans. Divide the dough in half and shape into a bread loaf. Put one loaf in each pan. Cover with a damp towel and let rise in a warm area for 45 minutes.

Cook: Preheat oven to 375°F. Bake for 40 to 45 minutes until brown and the loaves sound hollow when tapped. Transfer the loaves from the bread pans onto wire racks and allow to cool.

Sourdough French Bread

1 cup sourdough starter	2 tsp. sugar	2 tsp. salt
4 cups flour	1.5 cups warm water	1 pkg. yeast (optional)
2 cups flour (for kneading)	1/2 tsp. baking soda	

Preparation: If you are going to start this bread the evening before or early in the morning then you won't need the yeast. If you start it 3 hours before dinner then you will need the yeast. Mix the starter, water, and 4 cups flour in a bowl. Put this in a warm place and ignore it for the rest of the day. By evening it should have doubled and smell like your starter again. Mix the sugar, salt, baking soda and 1 cup of flour together. Sprinkle them over the dough and mix well. Turn the dough out onto your bread board and knead it, using the remaining flour. Shape loaves and place them on lightly greased cookie sheets. Let rise until doubled in bulk.
Cook: Slash tops of loaves, brush them with water or a well-beaten egg, and place in 400°F oven. (A pan of water on the lower shelf of the oven can help make a crispy crust.) Bake until medium dark brown.

Sourdough Biscuits

1 cup sourdough starter	1/3 cup sugar	1.5 tsp. salt
5 cups flour, sifted	1 cup lukewarm water	1 pkg. dry yeast

Preparation: Pour the yeast into a deep pan, then add water and dissolve. Stir and add sugar, salt, and starter and mix. Add flour and stir into batter dough. Cover dough with cloth and set in warm place to rise. When dough is double in volume you are ready. Turn the dough out on a floured surface and roll out 3/4 inch thick and cut into biscuits. Place in a baking pan which has about 1/8 inch melted shortening in it (or use bacon grease for a unique delicious flavor.) Dip both sides of each biscuit in melted shortening or bacon grease. Set aside and let rise in a warm place until doubled in volume.
Cook: Bake at 425°F for 15 to 20 minutes.
Variation: The recipe also makes delicious scones.

Sourdough Pancakes

2 cups flour	1 tbsp. warm butter or oil	1/2 cup lukewarm water
1 tbsp. honey	1/2 cup water	1 pkg. dry yeast

Preparation: Prepare the pancake batter the evening before. Dissolve yeast in 1/2 cup lukewarm water. Add the honey and let stand until bubbly (about 10 minutes). Add the butter, flour, and the rest of the water. Blend well. Cover. Let rise overnight in a warm spot.
Cook: In the morning, stir the batter. Drop 1/3 cup of batter on a hot oiled grill or pan. Fry each side until golden brown.

Chapter Fourteen

Bagels, Pretzels, Crackers, Chips, and Cheese Snacks
(No Eggs Required)

Whole Wheat Bagels (12 Bagels)

4 cups wheat flour	3 tbsp. sugar	1 tbsp. salt
1/2 pkg. yeast (1/2 tbsp.)	1.5 cups warm water	

Preparation: Dissolve yeast in warm water and let stand 12 minutes. Mix the flour, sugar, and salt together and then add the yeast water. Stir to make a moderately stiff dough. Turn onto a floured surface and knead until smooth. Cover and let rest for 15 minutes. Cut into 12 portions. Shape into small balls. Punch a hole in each ball with your finger. Pull gently to enlarge hole. Work into a uniform bagel shape. Cover and let rise 20 minutes.

Cook: In a large kettle combine 1 gallon of water and 1 tbsp. sugar and bring to a boil. Reduce heat to a simmer. Cook 4 or 5 bagels at a time for 7 minutes turning only once. Drain and place on a greased baking sheet. Bake at 375°F for 30 to 35 minutes. Remove from oven and allow to cool.

Whole Wheat Pretzels (12 Pretzels)

1.75 cups wheat flour	2 tsp. baking soda	1/4 tsp. salt
1/2 pkg. yeast (1/2 tbsp.)	3/4 cup warm water	1/4 cup cold water

Preparation: Dissolve yeast in warm water and let stand 12 minutes. Mix in flour. Knead dough for 10 minutes. Cover and let rise for 15 minutes. Divide dough into 12 pieces. On a floured surface, roll each piece into a rope 12" to 15" long. Lay one rope in a U-shape. Cross and twist the two ends one time and then press each end into the bottom of the U-shape at the 5 and 7 o'clock positions. Repeat with the other ropes. Dip pretzels into a solution of 1/4 cup cold water and 2 tsp. baking soda. Place dipped pretzel onto a greased cookie sheet. Sprinkle with a small amount of salt.

Cook: Bake at 400°F for 15 minutes.

Whole Wheat Crackers

1 cup wheat flour	1/4 cup cornmeal	1/4 tsp. salt
1 tsp. baking powder	1/2 cup butter	4 tbsp. milk

Preparation: Sift wheat flour and cornmeal. Mix in other dry ingredients. Cut in butter. Add milk to make a stiff dough. Roll until flat about 1/8-inch thick. Cut into squares, triangles, diamonds, etc. Prick with small fork.

Cook: Bake on buttered cookie sheet 5 minutes at 375°F or until brown on the bottom. Turn crackers over with a spatula and bake 3 to 5 minutes longer until again brown on the bottom.

Graham Crackers

1.75 cups wheat flour	1/4 cup brown sugar	3/4 tsp. baking powder	1/8 tsp. salt
1/8 cup oil	1/6 cup instant dry milk	1/4 tsp. cinnamon (optional)	3/8 cup water

Preparation: Combine flour, salt, brown sugar, dry milk, and baking powder. If desired, add the optional cinnamon. Mix well. Mix oil and water together and then add to dry ingredients and mix will. Chill dough in refrigerator for 1-hour. Then transfer to a floured board. Divide dough into halves. On

waxed paper, roll each half to about 1/8-inch thick. Cut into 2-inch squares. Peel crackers off waxed paper and place on lightly oiled cookie sheet. Prick with a fork.
Cook: Bake at 375°F for 15 minutes or until golden brown.

Whole Wheat Chips

| 1 cup wheat flour | 2 cups water | 1 tsp. salt |

Preparation: Sift the wheat flour. Add the salt and water. Stir well. The thinner the batter mixture, the thinner the chips, and the more evenly they will cook. Put the mixture into a used, empty, clean plastic ketchup (or mustard) squirt bottle. Squirt the mixture onto a non-stick cookie sheet in a thin potato chip shape.
Cook: Bake at 350°F for 10 to 15 minutes or until crisp. Check the chips after about 8 minutes and turn the chips over if the middle of the chip is not cooking as fast as the outside edges.
Variation: Use 1 tsp. Onion Salt instead of the regular salt.
Variation: Use 1 tsp. Garlic Salt instead of the regular salt.
Optional: Add 3 tbsp. grated Parmesan cheese.

Cheddar Cheese Crackers

1.5 cups wheat flour	1/4 tsp. baking soda	1/4 tsp. salt
1/8 tsp. cayenne pepper	1.5 ounces cheddar cheese	1/4 tsp. cream of tartar
1/2 tsp. light corn syrup	1/3 cup warm water	2 tbsp. shortening

Preparation: Mix one cup flour and all dry ingredients and the cheese (powder or grated). Stir to mix well. In a separate bowl mix the corn syrup and water and add the shortening and stir. The mixture will be quite heavy. Gradually add the flour mixture to form a dough that can be kneaded. On a floured surface, knead the dough 4 minutes by hand. Add more flour as necessary. Place dough in bowl, cover, and refrigerate at least one hour.
Preheat: Preheat oven to 400°F for 20 minutes before baking.
Shaping: Divide dough in half, keeping one-half covered in the refrigerator (until other half is removed from oven). Press and roll dough with your hands and a rolling pin to the length of your baking sheet. Roll to a thickness of 1/16 inch. Fold the dough from each end to the center to make 3 layers. Turn the dough over and roll it again to 1/16 inch thick. Lift the dough and place on the greased baking sheet. Prick the entire surface with a fork. Use a knife and score the dough into crackers of the desired size. Sprinkle lightly with salt.
Cook: Bake at 400°F for 8 to 15 minutes in center of oven until lightly brown and crisp. Remove and brush with melted butter (if available). Cool on wire racks. Break into crackers. Will stay fresh 3 to 4 weeks if stored in airtight container.

Cheese Wafers

1 cup flour	2 cups grated cheese	1/4 cup warm butter
1 tsp. salt	1/8 tsp. paprika (optional)	1/2 cup chopped nuts (optional)

Preparation: Combine all the above ingredients. Divide dough in half and form two long rolls. Place in the refrigerator for four-hours. Remove from the refrigerator and cut each roll into thin wafer slices.
Cook: Bake at 350°F for about 15 minutes in center of oven until lightly brown and crisp.

Chapter Fifteen

Oat Flour, Rice Flour, and Rye Flour (No Eggs Required)

Oat Flour

Put 1 cup of Quaker Oats (Quick or Old-Fashioned) through a grinder. Or blend for about one minute in a blender. Store in a tightly covered container in a cool dry place for up to six months. It has a sweet aroma and a nutty fresh flavor. Do **not** sift oat flour or you will lose some of its nutrients. May be used for baking, thickening, coating, or browning. If used in baking then substitute up to 1/3 oat flour for regular flour. Baked items will be more hearty, more tender, and a little more crumbly.

Rice Flour

Grind uncooked white rice into a fine powder. It can be used as a thickener or binder instead of flour. It is particularly useful for sauces. It can be cooked with milk and flavorings for a smooth dessert or added to biscuits to improve their texture. It can be used in equal amounts with wheat flour or cornmeal. Most people prefer a 1/4 to 1/3 ratio of rice flour to wheat flour.

Oatmeal Bread

3/4 cup rolled oats	3/4 cup boiling water	1 cup buttermilk	1 tbsp. salt
1/3 cup oil	1/2 cup warm water	1/2 cup honey	
5 cups flour	1/2 tsp. baking soda	1/2 pkg. yeast (1/2 tbsp.)	

Preparation: Dissolve yeast in 1/2 cup warm water and let stand 12 minutes. In a separate saucepan add the rolled oats to 3/4 cup boiling water. Cook for the time required for the type of oats you are using (quick or old-fashioned). Remove from heat. Add the buttermilk, oil, and honey. In a separate bowl, combine the flour, baking soda, and salt and mix well. Add the yeast solution to the flour mixture and stir well. Add the oat mixture and stir well. Knead on a board for about 10 minutes. Put in mixing bowl, cover, and let rise for 90 minutes. Punch down, divide in half, and form two loaves. Put one loaf in each bread pan. Let rise until double in bulk.
Cook: Bake at 375°F for 45 minutes.

Three-Grain Bread

2 cups cornmeal	4 cups boiling water	2 tsp. salt
2 cups wheat flour	1/2 cup warm water	1 tsp. sugar
2 cups rye flour	1/2 pkg. yeast (1/2 tbsp.)	

Variation: You may substitute either oat flour or rice flour for the rye flour.
Preparation: Dissolve yeast in 1/2 cup warm water with 1 tsp. sugar and let stand 12 minutes. To make a sponge, pour boiling water over cornmeal and salt in a large mixing bowl. Let it sit until the water is absorbed. Then stir in the yeast solution and 1 cup of rye flour. To set the sponge, cover the bowl and let it rest overnight in the refrigerator. The sponge will probably look flat but the yeast will have worked. Add the wheat flour and 1 cup rye flour to the sponge. Knead for 10 minutes. Divide dough in half. Grease two 8-9 inch pie plates or two 5"x9" loaf pans. Shape round loaves so that the dough covers the bottom of the pan. For rectangular loaves, roll out or flatten the divided dough into two 9-in. long cylinders, and fit them from end to end in each loaf pan. Set in a warm place to rise until double in bulk, about 2 hours.
Cook: Preheat the oven. Bake bread at 425°F for 45-50 minutes.

Chapter Sixteen

Simple Cornmeal Recipes (No Eggs Required)
All Recipes Use Regular Cornmeal and Not Self-Rising Cornmeal

Corn Bread

1 cup cornmeal	1/4 tsp. baking powder	1 tbsp. shortening	1/2 tsp. salt
2 tbsp. flour	1/4 tsp. baking soda	3/4 cup buttermilk	2 tsp. sugar

Optional: You may add 1 egg to the above recipe if you wish.
Preparation: Combine cornmeal, flour, baking powder, baking soda, sugar, and salt, and mix well. Add shortening and buttermilk. Stir until batter is smooth. Pour into a greased baking pan.
Cook: Bake 20 minutes at 450°F.

Corn Tortillas or Corn Chips or Taco Shells (7 six-inch Tortillas)

1 cup cornmeal	1/2 to 3/4 cups water	1/2 tsp. salt

Preparation: Combine cornmeal, salt, and 1/2 cup of water. Make a soft dough. If it is too dry, add a little more water. Cover with a cloth and let stand for 30 minutes. Shape the dough into 7 two-inch balls. Press (or roll) balls into flat 6-inch circles.
Tortillas Cook: Fry on hot griddle about 1 minute until edges start to curl. Flip and fry another minute.
Tortilla Corn Chips Cook: Deep fry small corn tortilla pieces for about 20 seconds in hot oil and remove with a slotted spoon and place on paper towel. Sprinkle with salt.
Taco Shells Cook: Heat 1/3 inch of oil in a skillet to 360°F. Slip an uncooked tortilla into the hot oil. After one second, use a spatula and fold the tortilla in half. Insert the spatula between the folds and press down and fry for 30 to 60 seconds until golden brown, then turn it over and repeat. Remove and drain curved side down so the oil will drip off. Fill with ground meat, refried beans, cheese, etc.

Hush Puppies

1 cup cornmeal	1/2 cup milk or water	1/2 tsp. salt
1/2 tsp. onion powder, onion flakes, or onion salt		1 tsp. baking powder

Mix all and shape into 1 inch balls. Deep fry in oil until well browned. Or make into cakes and pan fry.

Corn Pone

1 cup cornmeal	1/2 tsp. salt
3/4 cup hot water	1 tbsp. sugar, if available

Preparation: Mix everything and stir hard. Press into cakes about 1/2 inch thick.
Cook: Bake in Dutch oven 30 minutes. Or pan fry about 5 minutes on each side in a little hot fat or oil.

Pioneer Hoe Cakes

1 cup cornmeal	1/2 tsp. salt	hot water
2 tbsp. flour	1/4 tsp. baking powder	oil

Combine the salt, flour, cornmeal, and baking powder in a bowl. Add enough hot water to make a batter. Pour a little oil on the griddle. When it sizzles, add half the batter. Allow the cake to brown on one side. Then flip. An easy way to flip the cake is to put a plate on top of it, then lift the griddle and turn it upside down, holding the plate with the other hand. Add oil to the griddle and then slide the hoe cake, uncooked side down, back onto the re-oiled griddle. When done, repeat with the rest of the batter.

Cornmeal Mush and Polenta

| 1 cup cornmeal | 3.25 cups water | 1/2 tsp. salt |

Boil 2.25 cups water in heavy saucepan. In a separate bowl, mix the cornmeal, salt, and 1 cup cold water. Gradually add the cornmeal mixture to the boiling water, stirring well. Reduce heat, cover, and simmer 10 minutes, stirring occasionally to prevent scorching. (Or prepare in a double boiler.)

Cornmeal Mush Option: Continue simmering for an additional 20 minutes, stirring occasionally (or 30 minutes total simmering time). Serve hot with butter, or honey, or milk, or sugar, if available.

Polenta Bake Option: Pour hot cornmeal mixture into a greased 9-inch pie pan or cake pan and spread evenly. Bake at 450°F for 20 minutes. Allow to cool. Cut into wedges and serve with any type of sauce (pizza, spaghetti, taco, etc.), or cheese, or butter, or honey.

Polenta Fry Option: Pour hot cornmeal mixture into a bread loaf pan. Allow to cool. Chill in the refrigerator until firm. Remove from the bread pan and cut into half-inch thick slices. Fry each slice in melted butter for 5 minutes on first side, flip, and fry 5 minutes of other side, or until brown and crisp. Serve with butter, honey, or milk, if available.

Corn Dogs

| 1/2 cup cornmeal | 1/2 cup flour | 1 tsp. baking powder | 1/4 tsp. salt |
| 1 tbsp. sugar | 1 tbsp. shortening | 2 cans Vienna Sausage | 1/2 cup milk |

Preparation: Combine the cornmeal, flour, baking powder, salt, and sugar and mix well. Add the shortening and the milk. Stir into a smooth batter. Dip Sausages into the batter and coat generously.
Cook: Deep fry until golden brown.

Parched Corn

Dent corn (field corn) makes the best cornmeal. Sweet corn is best for snacks. Never use popcorn. Dry the corn indoors on the cobs. When dry, wrap your fist around the corn and twist your closed fist around the outside of the cob. The kernels should easily separate from the cob if the corn is dry enough.

Grease a skillet with a very light coating of olive oil (or vegetable oil, or bacon grease, or lard). Heat skillet over medium-low heat. Pour just enough dry corn into the hot skillet to barely cover the bottom of the skillet in one layer of corn, with a little space between the kernels. Each kernel needs to touch the bottom of the skillet. Continuously stir the corn (or shake the skillet) to prevent scorching. Depending on the heat, after 5 to 8 minutes the corn will swell into round kernels. Yellow corn should turn brown and white corn should turn a dark tan. It is better to cook just a little longer than not long enough. A few kernels may pop loudly but they will not puff up because you are not using popcorn. If a lot of kernels pop then the heat is too high. Pour the hot round kernels onto a paper towel and sprinkle with a little salt. Flip the kernels on the towel to remove the oil. When cool, store at room temperature in a plastic bag or a plastic container with a lid. The kernels will stay fresh a long time. Some uses of parched corn are:

1. **Quick Snack:** It is crunchy and easy to digest. If it is hard to bite then it was not cooked long enough.
2. **Granola Trail Mix:** Combine it with your favorite nuts, dried fruits, raisins, and/or pretzel pieces.
3. **Sweet Treat:** Mix it with a little brown sugar. (Caution: This can become an addictive sweet treat.)
4. **Complete Meal:** Mix it with cooked diced sweet peppers, onions, tomatoes, etc.
5. **Cornmeal:** Grind it into cornmeal.

Cornmeal Made from Parched Corn (Called Rockahominy or Pinole)

Grind parched corn in a grain grinder that is designed to grind corn kernels. If the texture of the ground cornmeal is not uniform, then sift it and grind the larger pieces of parched corn a second time.

1. Parched cornmeal can be used in almost any recipe in place of regular cornmeal.
2. It can be made into a healthy beverage by mixing a small amount of it with water and drinking it.
3. It has a lower moisture content than regular cornmeal and therefore it will remain fresh longer.
4. It digests and releases its energy slowly over a longer period of time. Therefore you will not get hungry as quickly when compared to eating the same food item made with regular cornmeal.

Chapter Seventeen

Wheat Berries

During serious famine conditions when food was extremely scarce people would **not** make bread. Instead they would sprout whatever wheat berries they had in order to increase both the volume and vitamins of their meals. Sprouted wheat weighs twice as much as wheat berries and it has three times the volume of wheat berries.

The sprouting directions below will work for wheat berries, beans, or seeds with the following adjustments to the sprouting times:

wheat berries - Allow 2 days.
sunflower seeds - Allow 2 to 3 days.
flax, lentil, mung, or soy beans - Allow 3 days.
alfalfa - Allow 4 or 5 days.

Wheat Sprouts

1. In the evening, put four ounces of wheat berries in the first jar (or plastic bag or container). Cover the wheat with water. Put the top on the container but don't tighten it. The wheat must have fresh air. Let it soak overnight. Drink the soak water the following morning (it is full of vitamins). Turn the container upside down and let it drain. Cover with a small towel to put the wheat in the dark. Four hours later, half fill the container with water, wait two minutes, drain and cover with a towel. (Note: If water is scarce then you can save the soak water and reuse it again each time you soak the berries.) Every 4 hours, half fill with water, wait 2 minutes, drain, and cover with a towel. The purpose is to keep the wheat moist but not water logged.
2. If all the extra water is **not** drained off the wheat berries then they will begin to ferment instead of sprouting.
3. Just before going to bed at the end of the day, start a second container with 4 ounces of wheat covered with water. You now have a system that will keep you in healthy, nutritious food every day.
4. The following day, fill both jars with water every 4 hours, wait 2 minutes, drain and cover. At the end of the day the wheat in the first jar will have small white sprouts extending from the ends of the kernels. It is part grain and part fresh vegetable. It has a high protein and vitamin content and it is a more complete food. Remove the sprouted wheat from the first jar and refill it with fresh grain and start the process over again.
5. Prepare the sprouted wheat using one of the cooking methods for wheat berry cereal (below).

Wheat Berry and Wheat Berry Sprout Recipes

Wheat Berry or Cracked Wheat Cereal (Pot Method) (Two Servings)

| 1 cup wheat berries | 4 cups water | 1 tsp. salt |

Combine the wheat berries and the water in a cook pot. Bring to a boil and cook for 2 minutes. Remove from heat, cover, and let stand for one hour. Return to heat and simmer for one hour. Eat it plain, or serve with milk, sugar, honey, or melted butter. If desired, add salt to taste.

Wheat Berry Cereal (Thermos Method) (One Serving)

| 1/2 cup wheat berries | 1 cup water | 1/2 tsp. salt |

Put wheat berries, salt, and water into a pot or saucepan and bring to a rolling boil, stirring the entire time. Quickly but carefully pour the contents from the pot through a wide mouth funnel into your thermos. Put the cap on the thermos firmly, but not too tightly, and lay the thermos on its side to evenly distribute the contents in the boiling hot water. Wait 8 hours or overnight. Pour the contents of the thermos into a bowl. Four ounces of dry wheat berries will yield about 12 ounces of cooked wheat and several ounces of vitamin and mineral enriched water. Be sure to drink the water. It has a pleasant taste and many valuable nutrients.

Wheat Berry Cereal (Microwave) (Two Servings)

| 1 cup wheat berries | 3 cups water | 1 tsp. salt |

Soak the wheat berries overnight. Then blend all of it on high for 20 to 30 seconds in a blender. Then cook it in the microwave for 3 to 5 minutes, stirring occasionally. Add milk and sugar to taste.

Chilled Wheat Berry Salad (Four Servings)

1 cup uncooked wheat berries	15 oz. can beans
2.5 cups water	15 oz. can mixed vegetables

Heat wheat berries in water until boiling in 2-quart saucepan, stirring occasionally. Reduce heat and simmer 50 to 60 minutes or until the wheat berries are tender but still chewy. Drain the berries. Mix with the beans and vegetables. Refrigerate for 2 hours to blend flavors and then serve.
Optional: Drip 2 tbsp. olive oil over salad before serving.

Popped Wheat

Soak wheat berries overnight in water and then spread them out on paper towels to dry. Then fry them in hot oil. It is easier if you use some sort of wire basket or strainer to dip into the hot oil instead of trying to remove them with a spoon. Season with either plain salt or with garlic salt.

Sautéed Sprouts

| 1 cup sprouts | 1 tbsp. butter | 1 tbsp. onion powder or flakes | 1 tsp. soy sauce |

Melt the butter in a saucepan. Add the onion powder and stir. Add the sprouts and stir gently. Stir in the soy sauce.

Simmered Sprouts

| 1 cup sprouts | 1 tbsp. butter | 1/2 cup water | 1/4 tsp. salt |

Add the salt to the water and heat. Add the sprouts and simmer for 5 minutes. Remove from heat and drain off the water. Add the butter and stir.

Nutritional Information for
Wheat Berries and Sprouted Wheat

Note: One ounce of wheat berries by weight is approximately equal to
One ounce of wheat berries by volume.

Serving Size:
Wheat Berries: Weight 1 ounce (28.4 grams)
Sprouted Wheat: Weight 2 ounces (56.8 grams)
(Weight Note: 1 ounce of Wheat Berries will yield 2 ounces of Sprouted Wheat by weight)
(Volume Note: 1 ounce of Wheat Berries will yield 3 ounces of Sprouted Wheat by volume)
(Average Analysis based on Several Samples)

Category Weight	Berry Amount 1 Ounce	Berry % RDV 1 Ounce	Sprout Amount 2 Ounces	Sprout % RDV 2 Ounces
Calories	97.1	5 %	113.3	6 %
Total Fat	0.6 g	1 %	0.7 g	1 %
Total Carbohydrate	21.5 g	8 %	24.3 g	9 %
Dietary Fiber	3.6 g	18 %	0.6 g	3 %
Protein	3.1 g	6 %	4.3 g	9 %
Cholesterol	0 mg	0 %	0 mg	0 %

Vitamins

Vitamin	Berry Amount	Berry % RDV	Sprout Amount	Sprout % RDV
Vitamin A	0 IU	0 %	0 IU	0 %
B1, Thiamin	0.117 mg	7 %	0.125 mg	8 %
B2, Riboflavin	0.031 mg	2 %	0.088 mg	5 %
B3, Niacin	1.362 mg	7 %	1.78 mg	9 %
B5, Pantothenic Acid	0.243 mg	2 %	0.55 mg	5.5 %
Vitamin B6	0.108 mg	5 %	0.15 mg	7.5 %
Vitamin B12	0 mcg	0 %	0 mcg	0 %
Vitamin C	0 mcg	0 %	0 mcg	0 %
Vitamin D	?	? %	?	? %
Vitamin E	0.411 mg	? %	0.028 mg	? %

Minerals

Mineral	Berry Amount	Berry % RDV	Sprout Amount	Sprout % RDV
Calcium, Ca	9.7 mg	0.9 %	16.0 mg	1.5 %
Copper, Cu	1.00 mg	50 %	0.15 mg	7.5 %
Iron, Fe	1.53 mg	7.5 %	1.23 mg	6 %
Magnesium, Mg	25.7 mg	6.5%	46.88 mg	11.8 %
Manganese, Mn	0.97 mg	48.5%	1.05 mg	52.5 %
Phosphorus, P	111.9 mg	12 %1	14.3 mg	12 %
Potassium, K	124.3 mg	3.2 %	96.58 mg	2.5 %
Selenium, Se	? Mg	? %	24.3 mg	34.8 %
Sodium, Na	0.57 mg	0.8 %	9.15 mg1	3.0 %
Zinc, Zn	1.00 mg	6.6 %	0.95 mg	6.3 %

Chapter Seventeen: Wheat Berries

Nutritional Information for Wheat Berries and Sprouted Wheat

Note: One ounce of wheat berries by weight is approximately equal to One ounce of wheat berries by volume.

(Continued from previous page.)

Amino Acids		
Amino Acid	**Berry Grams**	**Sprout Grams**
Alanine	?	0.168 g
Arginine	?	0.388 g
Aspartic Acid	?	0.258 g
Cystine	?	0.078 g
Glutamic Acid	?	1.070 g
Glycine	?	0.175 g
Histidine	?	0.113 g
Isoleucine	?	0.165 g
Leucine	?	0.290 g
Lysine	?	0.140 g
Methionine	?	0.068 g
Phenylalanine	?	0.20 g
Proline	?	0.385 g
Serine	?	0.195 g
Tryptophan	?	0.065 g
Threonine	?	0.145 g
Tyrosine	?	0.158 g
Valine	?	0.208 g
Other	**Other Berry**	**Sprout**
Ash	0.4 g	0.55 g
Folate	11.7 mcg	21.7 mcg

Chapter Eighteen

Grandpappy's Delicious Ice Cream Recipes
Using Instant Powdered Dry Milk
(An Ice Cream Churn is **Not** Required)
(One Large Serving for One Person)

Vanilla Ice Cream:
1/3 cup instant nonfat dry milk
1 cup hot water
1 teaspoon vanilla extract
3 tablespoon sugar (granulated or powdered)
1/4 teaspoon salt

Mix the dry milk with the hot water and then put it in the refrigerator overnight. The next day add the other ingredients and mix well. Put it in the freezer and allow it to chill. Stir the mixture every 30 minutes. Do **not** let the ice cream freeze solid. It is ready to eat when it is the consistency of soft-serve ice cream. Depending on the temperature of your freezer and how full your freezer is, the freezing process normally takes between 2 to 3 hours.

Variations:

Chocolate Ice Cream: Add 1 tablespoon cocoa powder **or** 1 tablespoon chocolate syrup at the same time the vanilla extract is added. Mix well so the chocolate is blended consistently throughout the mixture.

Fruit or Berry Ice Cream: After putting the ice cream mixture in the freezer, wait 90 minutes. Then add finely chopped/diced fresh peaches or strawberries or whole fresh blueberries to the freezer mixture just **before** it begins to harden. Stir well and then return the mixture to the freezer. This will help keep the fruit crisp tasting and prevent the fruit from becoming soggy.

Walnut or Pecan Ice Cream: After putting the ice cream mixture in the freezer, wait 90 minutes. Then add chopped/crushed walnuts or pecans to the freezer mixture just **before** it begins to harden. Stir well and then return the mixture to the freezer. This will help keep the nuts chewy and prevent them from becoming soggy.

Optional Ice Cream Churn: If you have an Ice Cream Churn, crushed ice, and rock salt, then follow the directions for making ice cream that accompany your churn. You will need to increase the above quantities in order to more fully utilize the capacity of your ice cream churn.

Chapter Nineteen

A Collection of
Easy Cake and Frosting Recipes
(No Eggs Required)

Decorative Icing Suggestions

Gently push cookie cutter shapes into the top icing on a cake or cupcake and then remove it to leave a small depression in the icing. Fill the depression with a contrasting color icing, or chocolate syrup, or colored confections.

Apple Cake

| 2 cups bread crumbs | 1 tbsp. sugar | 1/2 cup butter |
| 2.5 cups tart applesauce | 1 cup whipping cream | 2 tbsp. jam for decoration |

Brown crumbs with sugar and butter. Alternate layers of crumbs and applesauce in serving dish. Refrigerate. Top with whipped cream and dabs of jelly. For a crunchy cake, serve immediately. The crumbs will get moist the longer they sit.

Shortcake

| 2 cups wheat flour | 3 tbsp. sugar | 3 tsp. baking powder | 1 tsp. salt |
| 4 tbsp. shortening or butter | 1/2 cup milk | 1/2 cup water | |

Preparation: Sift wheat flour, add sugar, baking powder, and salt, and sift again. Work shortening into the dry mixture. Add liquid all at once and mix quickly just enough to dampen the dry mixture thoroughly. Spread into a round or square pan.
Cook: Bake at 400°F for 15 minutes. When done, cut into squares, split open, and spread with butter, honey, jam, or fruit.

Hard Cake

| 2 cups wheat flour | 1 cup sugar | 1 tsp. salt |
| 1/3 cup shortening or butter | 1/2 cup milk | 2.5 tsp. baking powder |

Preparation: Mix flour, sugar, baking powder, and salt. Cut in shortening to make fine crumbs. Remove about 1/2 cup crumbs and reserve them for the top of the cake. Add milk to the remaining crumbs. Mix briefly. Pat into a greased 9-inch pie pan. Top with the reserved crumbs.
Cook: Bake at 350°F for 30 minutes. Served topped with honey or diced fresh fruit.
Variation: Decrease sugar to 2 tbsp. and increase milk to 1 cup. Do not remove 1/2 cup crumbs for topping.

Easy Chocolate Cake

| 2 cups flour | 1 cup sugar | 1 tsp. baking soda |
| 1 cup oil | 1 cup water | 3 tbsp. cocoa |

Preparation: Mix all above ingredients. Pour batter into a rectangular cake pan.
Cook: Bake at 350°F for 25 to 30 minutes.
Optional Icing: Mix one cup granulated sugar with one cup water. Add nuts or anything else you can find to the Icing.

Chapter Nineteen: Cakes and Frostings

Basic Chocolate Cake

3 cups flour	2 cups sugar	2 tsp. baking soda
6 tbsp. cocoa	1/4 tsp. salt	1 tbsp. vanilla extract
2 tbsp. vinegar	3/4 cup oil	2 cups cold water

Preparation: Mix the flour, sugar, soda, cocoa, and salt in a large bowl. Add the vanilla extract, vinegar, and oil. Mix well. Gradually add the cold water. Pour cake batter into a two round cake pans or one rectangular cake pan.

Cook: Bake at 350°F for 25 to 30 minutes. Allow to cool. If desired you may add a Creamy Chocolate Frosting (see recipe below).

Confectioners Frosting I (Two-layer 8-inch Diameter Cake)

2.5 cups confectioners sugar	3 tbsp. hot water	2 drops food coloring (optional)

Put the hot water and food coloring in a small bowl and beat in the confectioners sugar until the frosting is thick enough to spread. Continue to beat for several minutes until very creamy.

Confectioners Frosting II (Two-layer 8-inch Diameter Cake)

2 cups confectioners sugar	1/3 cup shortening	1/8 tsp. salt
2 tbsp. milk	2 drops food coloring (optional)	

Cream the shortening and the salt together. Add the sugar and stir briskly. Stir in the milk and food coloring and beat well, adding more sugar or milk if necessary to get an easily spreadable consistency.

Confectioners Frosting III (Two-layer 8-inch Diameter Cake)

2 cups confectioners sugar	1/3 cup butter	1 tsp. vanilla extract
2 tbsp. milk	2 drops food coloring (optional)	

Add the sugar, butter, and vanilla extract. Stir in the milk and food coloring and beat well, adding more sugar or milk if necessary to get an easily spreadable consistency.

Confectioners Butter Frosting

1.5 cups confectioners sugar	1/3 cup butter	1 tsp. vanilla extract
1.5 tbsp. hot water	2 drops food coloring (optional)	

Melt butter over low heat until golden brown. Add optional food coloring, if desired. Add confectioners sugar and vanilla. Slowly add between 1 to 2 tbsp. of hot water until the frosting is of spreading consistency.

Creamy Chocolate Frosting

2.5 cups confectioners sugar	1/4 cup cocoa	1 tsp. vanilla extract
6 tbsp. softened butter	6 tbsp. milk	1 tbsp. light corn syrup or honey (optional)

In medium bowl, stir together confectioners sugar and cocoa and set aside. In large bowl, beat butter until creamy. Add 1/2 cup powered sugar mixture, corn syrup, and vanilla, beating until well blended. Add remaining powdered sugar mixture alternately with milk until of spreading consistency.

Variation: Add 1/2 cup chopped nuts.

Chapter Nineteen: Cakes and Frostings

Peanut Butter Chocolate Frosting

Add 1/4 cup peanut butter to the Creamy Chocolate Frosting Recipe on the previous page.

Caramel Icing I

1 cup brown sugar	1/3 stick butter
1 box confectioners sugar	1/3 cup milk

Put the brown sugar, butter, and milk in a saucepan. Stir. Bring to a hard boil. Remove from the heat and allow to cool. Add 1 box of confectioners sugar and stir until smooth.

Carmel Icing II

3/4 cup dark brown sugar	1/2 cup butter
2 cups granulated sugar	3/4 cup milk or cream

Combine all ingredients in a large saucepan and bring to a hard boil. Remove from heat. Continue to stir until smooth.

Granulated Sugar Icing

2 tbsp. flour	1 cup milk	1 cup butter
1 cup granulated sugar	1 tsp. vanilla extract	

In a saucepan, combine the flour and the milk. Heat until the mixture thickens. Allow to cool.
In another bowl, cream the butter, sugar, and vanilla extract and beat until fluffy. Add the cool milk mixture and continue beating until all the sugar is dissolved (this takes some time).

Granulated Sugar Topping

White granulated sugar can be colored with food coloring and a little water. Then allow it to dry. It may then be added as a sprinkle topping to any cake, cookie, or pie.

Cinnamon Sugar Sprinkle

1 tbsp. granulated sugar	1/4 tsp. cinnamon

Mix together and use as a sprinkle on cakes or cookies or muffins or biscuits.

Chapter Nineteen: Cakes and Frostings

Chapter Twenty

Simple Cookie Recipes (No Eggs Required)

Fresh eggs aren't always available and it is extremely difficult to find a good cookie recipe that doesn't include one or more eggs in the recipe. The recipes in this chapter don't require eggs to make delicious cookies. However, if you have eggs then you may add one egg to any of the following recipes.

Basic Cookie Recipe and Sugar Cookies (42 Cookies)

2 cups flour	1/2 cup shortening	1 tsp. salt
1 cup granulated sugar	1 tsp. baking powder	1 tsp. vanilla extract (optional)

Preparation: Combine the flour, baking powder, and salt. In another bowl, cream the shortening and the sugar. Blend in the vanilla extract. Gradually blend in the dry ingredients. If the final dough is too dry, then add just a little water to make the dough stick together. Pinch off walnut sized pieces of dough and roll into balls. Roll balls in some granulated sugar and place 1.5" apart on a lightly greased baking sheet. Flatten each ball with the bottom of a glass dipped in water and then in granulated sugar.
Cook: Bake at 350°F for 10 to 12 minutes or until lightly colored. Transfer to a wire rack to cool.
Variations: Don't coat outside with granulated sugar. Substitute almond extract or any flavoring for the vanilla extract. Or use nuts or raisins. The dough can be rolled into balls and baked as is or it can be flattened. Or you can roll pieces of the dough into ropes and make rings, twists, or braids.

Shortbread Cookies (54 Small Cookies)

2.25 cups flour	1 cup shortening
1.25 cups light brown sugar	1 tsp. vanilla extract

Optional Ingredient: 1/2 cup ground walnuts, pecans, or almonds.
Preparation: In a large bowl, cream the shortening and brown sugar. Beat in the vanilla extract. Gradually blend in the flour. (Mix in the nuts if available.) Pinch off walnut sized pieces of dough and roll into 1" balls. Place 1.5" apart on ungreased baking sheet. Flatten with the back of a spoon dipped in flour.
Cook: Bake at 350°F for 10 to 15 minutes or until lightly colored. Transfer to a wire rack to cool.

Fruit Preserves Cookies (60 Small Cookies)

2 cups flour	1 cup butter
1/2 cup powdered sugar	1/2 cup fruit preserves

Preparation: In a medium bowl, cream the butter and powdered sugar. Gradually blend in the flour. Pinch off large olive size pieces of dough and roll into balls. Place 1" apart on ungreased baking sheet and make an indentation in the center of each cookie with your finger. Fill the hollow indentation with a small amount of fruit preserves.
Cook: Bake at 375°F for 15 to 18 minutes, or until lightly colored. Transfer to a wire rack to cool.

Crescent Cookies (36 Cookies)

2 cups flour	1 cup butter, room temperature	1/2 cup powdered sugar
2 tsp. vanilla extract	1 cup ground nuts (optional)	

Preparation: Combine all ingredients in a large bowl. (Fold in the optional nuts.) Shape into crescents (or balls) and place 1.5" apart on a lightly greased baking sheet.
Cook: Bake at 350°F for 20 minutes or until lightly colored. Transfer to wire racks to cool.

Welsh Scones (36 Cookies)

1.5 cups flour	6 tbsp. shortening	1/3 cup milk	1/4 tsp. salt
3 tbsp. granulated sugar	1 tsp. baking soda	1 tsp. cream of tartar	

Option: 2 tsp. of baking powder may be substituted for the baking soda and the cream of tartar.
Preparation: Combine the flour, baking soda, cream of tartar, and salt. In a large bowl, cream the shortening and the sugar. Beat in the milk. Gradually blend in the dry ingredients. On a floured surface, roll out the dough until 1/2 inch thick. Cut into 3" or 4" round circles. Cut each circle into 6 wedges and place 1" apart on 2 lightly greased baking sheets.
Cook: Bake at 375°F for 15 to 20 minutes or until lightly colored. Transfer to a wire rack to cool.

Dutch Cookies (48 Small Cookies)

1.5 cups flour	1/2 tsp. baking soda	1/4 tsp. salt
1/2 cup powdered sugar	1/8 cup granulated sugar	1/2 cup butter (room temperature)

Preparation: Cream butter and powdered sugar until smooth. Add flour, baking soda, and salt and beat until smooth. Roll the dough into a 12" long roll that looks like a long sausage. Wrap in some wax paper and refrigerate for one hour.
Cook: Preheat oven to 350°F. Slice cookies from the roll about 1/4 inch thick on a diagonal and place on an ungreased cookie sheet. Bake for 15 minutes or until cookies are golden brown. Allow cookies to cool about 3 minutes before removing them from the cookie sheet.

Swedish Butter Cookies (42 Cookies)

2 cups flour	3/4 cup butter, room temperature	1/2 tsp. salt
3/4 cup granulated sugar	1 tsp. baking powder	1 tsp. vanilla extract
3/4 cup powdered sugar	1/2 cup ground nuts (optional)	

Preparation: Combine the flour, baking powder, and salt. In a large bowl, cream butter with the two sugars. Beat in the vanilla extract. Gradually blend in the dry ingredients. (Fold in the nuts.) Drop dough by spoonfuls 1.5" apart on a lightly greased baking sheet.
Cook: Bake at 350°F for 12 to 14 minutes or until lightly colored. Transfer to wire racks to cool.

Scottish Butter Cookies (30 Cookies)

1.5 cups flour	1/4 tsp. salt (optional)
1/2 cup sugar (granulated, powdered, or brown)	1/4 cup corn starch (optional)
1/2 cup butter, room temperature	1/2 tsp. vanilla extract (optional)

Preparation: Stir the sugar into the flour. Gradually add the soft butter. (If available, add any or all of the optional ingredients: salt, corn starch, and vanilla extract.) Chill the dough in the refrigerator. Roll the dough down flat to a thickness of 1/2 inch, or a little less. Cut into shapes using cookie cutters (or form into shapes using your fingers, such as ovals, squares, triangles, or any other shape that pleases you). If desired, you may flute the edges like a pie crust. Place on an ungreased cookie sheet.
Cook: Bake at 325°F for about 20 minutes. Transfer to wire racks to cool.
Optional: Sprinkle tops of cookies with a little sugar while they still hot.

Chapter Twenty: Cookies

Honey Cookies (42 Cookies)

2.5 cups flour	1/2 cup shortening	1/2 tsp. salt
1 cup honey	1 tsp. baking soda	1 tbsp. ginger

Preparation: Combine the flour, baking soda, ginger, and salt. In a large saucepan melt the shortening with honey, stirring until smooth. Remove from heat and gradually blend in the dry ingredients, stirring until the dough is smooth and no longer sticky. On a well floured surface, roll out the dough until 1/4 inch thick. Using cooking cutters, cut out cookies and place 1 inch apart on a lightly greased baking sheet.
Cook: Bake at 350°F for 12 to 15 minutes, or until lightly colored. Transfer to a wire rack to cool.

Honey Wheat Cookies (36 Cookies)

1.25 cups wheat flour	1/2 cup oil	1/4 tsp. cinnamon
1/2 cup honey	2 tsp. baking powder	1/4 tsp. vanilla extract
1/4 cup milk	1/2 tsp. baking soda	

Preparation: Mix all ingredients. Drop onto a greased cookie sheet by teaspoonfuls.
Cook: Bake at 350°F for 10 minutes, or until lightly colored. Transfer to a wire rack to cool.

Pecan Sandies

2 cups sifted flour	1.5 tbsp. powdered sugar	1 cup butter
1 cup chopped pecans	2 tsp. vanilla extract	1 tsp. water

Preparation: Cream butter and sugar together. Add the flour and stir well. Add the chopped pecan, vanilla extract, and water and stir well. Roll the mixture into balls. Flatten or shape as desired. Place on a greased cookie sheet.
Cook: Bake in preheated 350°F oven for 10 to 12 minutes. Sprinkle each cookie with a little powdered sugar. Allow to cool.

Snowball Cookies I

2.25 cups flour	3/4 cup nuts, finely chopped	1/4 tsp. salt
1/2 cup powdered sugar	1 tsp. vanilla extract	1 cup butter

Preparation: Cream butter, powdered sugar, and vanilla. Stir in remaining ingredients. Chill dough. Roll dough into 1" balls and put on ungreased cookie sheet.
Cook: Bake at 400°F for 10 to 12 minutes. (Don't brown them.) While still warm, roll them in powdered sugar. Cool on rack and then roll in powdered sugar again.

Snowball Cookies II

1 cup flour	1 cup ground nuts	1/2 cup butter
2 tbsp. granulated sugar	1/4 cup powdered sugar	1 tsp. vanilla

Preparation: Cream the butter, granulated sugar, and vanilla. Add the flour, and nuts. Mix well. Chill dough. Roll dough into 1" balls and put on ungreased cookie sheet.
Cook: Bake at 300°F for 30 minutes. While still warm, roll them in powdered sugar. Cool on rack and then roll in powdered sugar again.

Oatmeal Cookies (54 Cookies)

2 cups flour	1 cup shortening	1 tsp. salt
1 cup light brown sugar	1 tsp. baking soda	3/4 cup milk
1 cup rolled oats	1/2 tsp. nutmeg	

Preparation: Combine the flour, oats, baking soda, nutmeg, and salt. In a large bowl, cream the shortening and brown sugar. Beat in the milk. Gradually blend in the dry ingredients. Cover and chill for 2 hours. On a floured surface, roll out the dough until 1/4 inch thick. Use cookie cutters and cut out cookies and place 1" apart on a lightly greased baking sheet.
Cook: Bake at 350°F for 10 to 12 minutes or until golden. Transfer to wire racks to cool.

Boiled Oatmeal Cookies

1 cup granulated sugar	4 tbsp. butter	1/8 tsp. salt
1.5 cup quick oats	1/4 tsp. vanilla extract	1/4 cup milk

Variation: Peanut Butter Oatmeal Cookies: Add 1/4 cup peanut butter when you add the quick oats.
Variation: Chocolate Oatmeal Cookies: Add 2 tbsp. cocoa when you add the quick oats.
Variation: Chocolate Peanut Butter Oatmeal Cookies: Add 2 tbsp. cocoa **and** 1/4 cup peanut butter when you add the quick oats.
Variation: Raisins or Nuts: Add either 1/4 cup raisins or 1/4 cup nuts after removing the mixture from the heat. Stir well.
Preparation: Combine the sugar, butter, milk, and salt in a medium size saucepan.
Cook: Bring to a rolling boil. Reduce heat and boil for an additional 3 minutes, stirring constantly. Add the quick oats and the vanilla extract (and the optional peanut butter and/or cocoa). Continue to boil and stir until thick (about 1.5 minutes). Remove from heat. (Add the optional raisins or nuts and stir well.) Drop with a tablespoon onto wax paper and make a round cookie about 1.5 inches in diameter. Allow to cool.

Chapter Twenty-One

Easy Pie and Cobbler Recipes

Decorative Pie Crust Patterns

To make decorative pie crust edges, you may do any of the following:

1. Use a spoon to produce a scalloped edge.
2. Use a fork to produce a crosshatch or herringbone pattern.
3. Use an old-fashioned can opener to produce a series of sharp points around the outside edge.
4. Instead of a solid top crust, you can places strips of dough 3/4-inch wide and about 1-inch apart across the top of the pie in a criss-cross pattern.

9-Inch Pie Crust

2 cups flour	3/4 tsp. salt
2/3 cup shortening or oil or lard	4 to 6 tbsp. ice cold water (or cold milk)

Sift flour and salt together and cut in shortening. Add water gradually until mixture will hold together. Divide dough in half. Roll both pieces on a floured board to the desired size. Line a 9-inch (or 10-inch) pie pan with one piece of dough being careful **not** to stretch the dough.

After filling the lower pie crust with the desired filling according to the pie recipe you are using, dampen the edges of the lower crust with a little cold water. Cut short slits in the remaining piece of dough with a sharp knife to allow steam to escape during baking. Place the remaining piece of dough over the filled pie. Press the edges of the two pieces of dough together using a fork or your fingers. Flute the edges if desired. Bake the pie according to the directions in your pie recipe.

Optional: Instead of rolling the dough into two circles, gather one-half the dough for the bottom crust and put it into a pie pan. Then press the dough evenly to the sides of pie pan first and then to the bottom of the pan.

Optional: You may add two tablespoons of granulated sugar at the same time you add the salt in the above recipe.

Note: Some pie recipes require the lower pie crust to be lightly browned for about 10 minutes in a 450°F oven before adding the pie filling.

Note: Using lard instead of shortening or oil will yield a superior quality pie crust.

Rich Southern Pastry

Increase shortening in above recipe to 1 cup. If you chill the dough before rolling then it will make the pastry easier to handle.

Easy Pie Crust

1.5 cups flour	1 tbsp. sugar	3/4 tsp. salt
1/2 cup oil	2 tbsp. cold milk (or cold water)	

Put the flour, sugar, and salt into a pie pan and mix well.

In a separate cup, mix the oil and milk together until creamy. The pour the liquid into the flour mixture inside the pie pan. Mix together until crumbly. Press mixture evenly to the sides of pie pan first and then to the bottom of the pan. Fill and bake according to pie recipe instructions.

Graham Cracker Pie Crust

| 1 cup wheat flour | 1 tbsp. brown sugar | 1/2 cup butter | 1/2 tsp. salt |

Preparation: Mix all the above ingredients to form a soft dough. Press the dough mixture into the bottom and sides of a pie pan.
Cook: Bake at 350°F for 15 minutes. Remove from oven and allow to cool. Then follow the appropriate pie recipe instructions.

Fruit Preserves Pie (Using One 10-inch Pizza Pan)

| 1 Rich Southern Pastry (recipe on page 48) | 2 cups of fruit preserves |

Fruit Preserves Options: Apple, Pear, Peach, Cherry, Strawberry, Blueberry, Raspberry, or Blackberry Preserves (or Jelly).
Preparation: Follow the "Rich Southern Pastry" recipe on page 48. Roll all of the pastry dough into one 10-inch round flat circle and place it on a 10-inch pizza pan. The outer edges of the circle should be a little thicker than the rest of the dough.
Cook: Bake in 375°F oven for 6 minutes. Remove from oven. Spread the contents of two cups of fruit preserves evenly over the flat pie crust. Bake an additional 4 to 6 minutes until underside of crust is golden brown.

Berry or Fruit Pie

4 cups berries	1.5 tbsp. lemon juice	1/8 tsp. salt
1 cup sugar	2 tbsp. flour	1 pie crust

Preparation: Mix sugar, flour, and salt. Add lemon juice. Add berries. Pour mixture into pie crust. Cover with top crust.
Cook: Bake at 450°F for 10 minutes. Reduce heat to 350°F and bake 20 to 30 minutes longer.
Blueberry, Huckleberry: Follow above recipe.
Blackberry: 3 cups berries. Follow above recipe.
Peach: 8 sliced peaches. No lemon juice. Follow above but bake 35 minutes at end.
Apple: 6 peeled, sliced apples. No lemon juice. Follow above but bake 45 minutes at end.

Shoo Fly Pie

2 cups flour	1 pie crust bottom	1 tsp. baking soda	1/2 cup sugar
1 cup corn syrup	1 cup warm water	1/3 cup shortening or butter	

Preparation: Sift flour and sugar together. Add shortening to make fine crumbs. In a separate bowl, combine corn syrup and baking soda with 1 cup warm water. Fill pie crust with alternating layers of corn syrup and crumb mixture, ending with crumbs on top.
Cook: Bake at 425°F for 10 minutes. Then reduce heat to 350°F and bake until filling is firm.

Fruit Cobbler (using Fresh Fruit)

1.75 cups flour	1 tbsp. baking powder	6 tbsp. butter	1/2 tsp. salt
1/2 cup sugar	3/4 cup cream or milk	6 cups fresh fruit	

Preparation: Mix flour, baking powder, and salt in a large bowl. Add the butter. Add the sugar and mix well. Stir in the cream with a fork. Gather the dough and knead inside the bowl. Set aside. Preheat oven to 375°F. Grease a 9-inch by 13-inch baking pan. Sweeten the fruit to taste and put in the greased

pan. Roll the dough on a lightly floured surface to fit the top of the baking pan. Place on top of fruit.
Cook: Bake at 375°F for 40 to 50 minutes until lightly browned and a toothpick comes out clean when inserted in the crust.

Fruit Cobbler (using Canned Fruit)

1 cup flour	6 tbsp. butter	1 tsp. vanilla extract (optional)
1 cup sugar	1 cup milk	1 large 25 oz. can fruit

Option One: Crust on Bottom.
Preparation: Melt butter in medium baking dish. Then mix in flour, sugar, milk, and optional vanilla extract. Pour the can of fruit over this mixture and do **not** stir.
Cook: Bake at 350°F for 50 to 60 minutes.

Option Two: Crust on Top.
Preparation: Pour fruit into bottom of 9 x 12 baking pan. Mix the flour, sugar, milk, and optional vanilla extract in a separate bowl and then pour over the fruit. Do **not** stir. Cut butter into slices and place on top of the mixture.
Cook: Bake at 350°F for 45 minutes. When done you may sprinkle the top with sugar (optional).

Blueberry (or Huckleberry) Crisp

1/3 cup wheat flour	4 cups blueberries	1/3 cup water	2 tsp. lemon juice
3/4 cup uncooked oatmeal	4 tbsp. butter	1/3 cup sugar	

Preparation: Wash the berries. Remove stems and any unripe berries. Place the berries in an 8-inch square baking pan. Pour in the water and the lemon juice and stir well. In a mixing bowl, cream the butter and sugar together. Combine the flour and the uncooked oatmeal. Mix until crumbly. Sprinkle the mixture over the blueberries.
Cook: Bake at 375°F for 40 to 45 minutes or until well browned.

Fried Pies (using Canned Pie Filling)

1 Rich Southern Pastry (recipe on page 48)	1 can of pie filling (20 to 26 ounces)
1 cup sugar (granulated or powdered)	2 tsp. cinnamon

Pie Filling Options: Apple, Cherry, Peach, Pear, or Berry Pie Filling, or use some Chocolate Pudding as a filling.
Preparation: Follow the "Rich Southern Pastry" recipe on page 48. Roll the pastry dough to a thickness of about one-quarter inch. Use an empty Crisco can (or any other empty 1-gallon food can) to cut circles from the dough. Place about 3 tablespoons of pie filling evenly onto one-half of one of the dough circles and fold the other half of the dough over the top of the pie filling. Use a fork to pinch the outer edges of the pie closed so the pie filling will not leak out. Continue filling each of the dough circles with pie filling until all the small pies are ready to be fried.
Cook: Heat some shortening, lard, or oil in a deep frying pan. You will need about 3/4 inch of melted shortening in the pan so the shortening will completely cover the pies when they are added. Depending on the size of your frying pan, use a spatula to place one, two, or three small pies carefully into the hot oil one at a time until the frying pan is almost full (only one layer of pies on the bottom of the pan). Fry until the pie crust turns a golden brown and then carefully transfer the fried pies to a cooling rack. While they are still hot, sprinkle the top of each pie with a light coating of sugar and then sprinkle with just a little cinnamon. Allow the pies to cool before eating.

Chapter Twenty-Two

Easy Candy and Fudge Recipes

Peanut Butter Candy Roll

3/4 cup smooth peanut butter	2 tbsp. milk
4 tbsp. (or 1/2 stick) soft butter	1/2 tsp. vanilla extract (optional)
2 cups confectioners sugar	4 drops food coloring (optional)

Put the milk, food coloring, and vanilla extract in a medium bowl. Add the soft butter and stir. Add the powdered sugar and mix to the consistency of pie dough. Divide dough into 2 portions. Chill the dough in the refrigerator to make the dough easier to spread. Roll each portion separately between sheets of wax paper. Spread each portion with smooth peanut butter and roll up like a jelly roll. Chill in the refrigerator for 2 to 3 hours. Then cut into 1/2-inch to 3/4-inch slices. Store uneaten candy in the refrigerator in an airtight plastic bowl with a lid.

Peanut Butter Candy I

1 cup peanut butter	1/2 pound butter	2 tbsp. vanilla extract
1 pound box confectioners sugar		3 tbsp. cocoa

In large saucepan, melt the butter and the peanut butter. Add the vanilla extract and the sugar and mix well. Add the cocoa. Stir until well blended. Pour mixture into a buttered pan (8-inch or 9-inch square). Chill until firm. Cut into pieces.

Peanut Butter Candy II

1/2 cup peanut butter	1/2 cup corn syrup or honey
1/2 cup powdered dry milk	1/2 cup confectioners sugar

In a large bowl, stir the corn syrup and peanut butter together until smooth. Add the dry milk and stir. Add the sugar and stir until well mixed. Pinch of some of the candy mixture and roll into 1-inch diameter balls. Chill in the refrigerator.

Peanut Butter Candy III

1/2 cup peanut butter	1 tsp. vanilla extract
3/4 cup milk	2 cups granulated sugar

Butter 8-inch square pan and set aside. Stir the sugar into the milk and bring to a boil. Continue to cook until the mixture forms a soft ball when a small amount is added to a cup of cold water. Stir in the vanilla extract and the peanut butter. Mix well and pour into the buttered pan. Cool until firm. Cut into squares.

Whole Wheat Peanut Butter Candy

1 cup peanut butter	1 cup butter	1 cup honey
1.5 cup whole wheat flour	1/2 cup chopped nuts (optional)	

Melt the butter, honey, and peanut butter in a saucepan. Stir in the flour and cook for five minutes. Remove from heat. Add nuts if desired. Allow to cool before eating.

Easy Peanut Butter Fudge (36 Pieces)

| 1 cup peanut butter | 2 cups granulated sugar | 1/2 cup water |

Butter 8-inch square pan and set aside. In heavy 3-quart saucepan, stir together sugar and water. Cook over medium heat, stirring constantly, until mixture boils. Add the peanut butter. Stir to prevent burning. Continue to cook on medium heat until the mixture pulls away from the pan. Pour into prepared buttered pan. Cool until firm. Cut into squares.

Peanut Butter Fudge (36 Pieces)

1/2 cup peanut butter	2/3 cup milk	2 tbsp. light corn syrup
2 cups granulated sugar	1 tbsp. butter	1 tsp. vanilla extract

Butter 8-inch square pan and set aside. In heavy 3-quart saucepan, stir together sugar, milk, and corn syrup. Cook over medium heat, stirring constantly, until mixture boils. Continue boiling, with stirring, to 234°F (about 30 minutes) or until syrup, when dropped in ice water, forms a soft ball which flattens when removed from the water and it is slightly chewy. (Bulb of thermometer should not rest on bottom of saucepan.) Add vanilla extract and peanut butter. Beat until mixture thickens, about 30 seconds. Quickly pour into prepared pan. Score into squares with a knife. Cool until firm. Cut into squares.

Chocolate Fudge (36 pieces)

Omit peanut butter in above recipe. Add 1/3 to 1/2 cup cocoa powder at first step with sugar, milk, and corn syrup. Increase milk from 2/3 to 1 cup.

Creamy Butter Fudge (36 pieces)

Omit peanut butter in above recipe. Increase the milk from 2/3 to 1 cup and increase butter from 1 tbsp. to 8 tbsp. (or 1 stick butter).

Extra Creamy Fudge

2 cups brown sugar	1/2 cup milk	1.5 tsp. baking powder	1/4 tsp. salt
3 tbsp. flour	2 tbsp. butter	1 tsp. vanilla extract	

Combine everything except vanilla extract and follow Peanut Butter Fudge recipe above. Add vanilla extract at the point specified in the above recipe.

Cocoa Fudge (1.5 pounds or 36 pieces)

3 cups granulated sugar	2/3 cup cocoa powder	1/8 tsp. salt
1/2 stick (or 1/4 cup) butter	1 tsp. vanilla extract	1.5 cups milk

Stir sugar, cocoa, and salt together in a large saucepan. Stir in the milk. Cook over medium heat until mixture boils stirring constantly. When mixture reaches a rolling boil, stop stirring but continue heating to 234°F (or until a drop of the mixture forms a soft ball when dropped into very cold water and then flattens when removed from the water). Remove from heat. Add the butter and the vanilla extract but do **not** stir. Allow to cool to 110°F or until lukewarm. Beat with a spoon until the fudge begins to thicken and lose some of its gloss. Quickly spread the fudge into a buttered 9-inch cake or pie pan. Allow to cool and then cut into squares.
Optional: Add chopped nuts after fudge cools to 110°F.

Chapter Twenty-Two: Candy and Fudge

Fantastic Fudge (36 pieces)
(A Fast Simple Recipe That Makes Perfect Fudge Every Time)

1 box (or 16 oz.) confectioners sugar	1/2 cup cocoa powder	1/8 tsp. salt
1 stick (or 1/2 cup) butter	2 tsp. vanilla extract	1/4 cup milk

Melt the butter in a large non-stick saucepan over medium-low heat. Then stir in the milk. Add the vanilla extract, confectioners sugar, cocoa, and salt and stir well. Continue to cook over medium-low heat for six-minutes stirring continuously. Remove from heat and allow to cool for two-minutes. Then pour into a buttered 8 or 9-inch cake or pie pan and spread the fudge evenly to the edges of the pan. Chill in the refrigerator for two hours. Slice the fudge into pieces approximately 1.5 inches square and transfer to a serving dish.

Optional: Add 1/2 cup chopped nuts after the fudge cools for two-minutes, stir, and then pour into the 8 or 9-inch pan and chill in the refrigerator.

Caramels

1 can evaporated milk	2 cups honey	1/4 tsp. salt
1 tsp. vanilla extract	3 tbsp. butter	1 cup chopped nuts (optional)

Cook the milk and the honey until it forms a firm ball (about 255°F). Stir in the butter, vanilla extract, salt, and optional nuts. Pour into a buttered pan. Allow to cool and cut into pieces.

Butterscotch Candy

2 cups brown sugar	2 tsp. vinegar	4 tsp. cold water	1/2 cup butter

Combine all ingredients and bring to a boil. Continue to boil until a hard ball is formed when a teaspoon of the mixture forms a hard ball when dropped in cold water. Pour mixture into an oiled pan and allow it to cool. Cut into candy size pieces.

Chapter Twenty-Two: Candy and Fudge

Chapter Twenty-Three
Sweet Treats

Peanut Butter Cookies with One Egg (42 Small Cookies)

1 1/3 cups flour	1 tsp. baking soda	1/2 tsp. salt
1/2 cup shortening	1/2 cup granulated sugar	1/2 cup light brown sugar
1/2 cup peanut butter	1 tsp. vanilla extract	1 egg

Preparation: Combine the flour, baking soda, and salt. In a large bowl, cream the vegetable shortening and the two sugars. Beat in the peanut butter. Beat in the vanilla extract and the egg. Gradually blend in the dry ingredients. Pinch off walnut sized pieces of the dough and roll into balls. Roll the balls in granulated sugar and place 1-inch apart on an ungreased baking sheet. If desired, use a wet fork to press the balls flat and form a criss-cross pattern in the top of the cookie.
Cook: Bake at 350°F for 11 to 13 minutes. Transfer to a wire rack to cool.
Optional: Press between one to three small chocolate chips into the top of each cookie immediately after they are removed from the oven.

Peanut Butter Balls

1/3 cup peanut butter	1/2 cup instant nonfat dry milk	1/4 cup honey

Combine all ingredients and shape into small balls about one-inch in diameter.

Cinnamon Rolls or Sweet Sticky Buns

3 cups flour	2.5 tbsp. instant dry milk	1/2 cup sugar	1/2 tsp. salt
1/2 pkg. yeast (1/2 tbsp.)	1 cup warm water	1/2 tsp. cinnamon	2.5 tbsp. oil

Preparation: Dissolve yeast in warm water and let stand 12 minutes. Then add sugar, salt, oil, dry milk, and 3/4 cup flour. Beat vigorously by hand. Stir in additional flour to make a stiff dough. Knead on a floured board until smooth and elastic (10 minutes). Place in greased bowl, cover, and let rise in a warm place for 45 minutes. Punch dough down. Let rise again about 20 minutes. Roll dough to 1/2 inch thickness. Cover and let rise 1 hour. Butter the top of the dough. Sprinkle with cinnamon and a little more sugar. Roll up the dough and slice into 1/2 widths. Place in individual greased muffin tins or onto a greased cookie pan.
Cook: Bake at 375°F for 15 minutes or until done.
Optional: Add raisins and/or nuts with the cinnamon.

Optional Icing for Above Cinnamon Rolls

2 tbsp. butter	1 cup sugar (brown or powdered)
1 or 2 tbsp. boiling water	2 tbsp. corn syrup or 1/2 tsp. vanilla extract

Cook butter until it stops bubbling and it is brown and foamy. Remove from heat. Add either the corn syrup or the vanilla extract but not both. Stir in the sugar. Gradually add the hot water to achieve the desired consistency for spreading.

Homemade Marshmallows

2 tbsp. gelatin	8 tbsp. cold water	1/4 tsp. salt
2 cups granulated sugar	2 tsp. vanilla extract	1/2 cup cold water

You will also need a little confectioners sugar to coat the outside of the marshmallows.
Preparation: Dust a 8-inch square pan with confectioners sugar. Set aside. In a small bowl, soak gelatin in 8 tbsp. of cold water. Set aside. Combine granulated sugar and 1/2 cup cold water in a large heavy saucepan.
Cook: Cook and stir over medium heat until dissolved. Add gelatin and bring to a boil. Remove from heat, pour into a large bowl and let stand until partially cool. Add vanilla extract and salt. Beat until soft and doubled in volume. Pour into the prepared pan to about 1/2-inch thick. Allow to cool until it will not stick to the finger. Cut into 1.5-inch pieces and roll in confectioners sugar. Or cut into 3/4-inch pieces for miniature marshmallows.

Caramel Syrup

1.5 cups granulated sugar	1/4 cup cold water	1/4 cup lemon juice
2 tbsp. unsalted butter	1/2 cup boiling water	

Combine the sugar, cold water, and lemon juice in a saucepan. Heat to boiling and stir until the sugar dissolves. Cook over medium-low heat, stirring occasionally, until the syrup turns a golden brown. Remove the pan from the heat. Protect your hand with a mitt and use a long-handled spoon, and stir in the boiling water and butter until well blended. Serve warm or at room temperature. The syrup will thicken as it cools but it can be thinned with a little more boiling water if necessary.

Popcorn

1/2 cup popcorn	1 tbsp. oil	1/2 tsp. salt

You will need the special variety of popcorn and not ordinary corn.
One-half cup of popcorn kernels will yield approximately one quart of popped corn.
Put the oil in the bottom of a covered skillet. Heat the oil over high heat. Add the popcorn and immediately put the cover on top of the skillet. Shake the popcorn inside the skillet to coat all the popcorn with the hot oil. Continue shaking the skillet the entire time you are popping the corn. After most of the popcorn has popped and two or three seconds have passed and you don't hear any more popping then turn off the heat but keep shaking the skillet. Remove the cover from the skillet and pour the popcorn into a bowl. Remove and discard any unpopped kernels. Sprinkle the salt over the popcorn.
Variation: Melt some butter in a separate sauce pan and dribble it over the hot popcorn.

Caramel Popcorn

8 cups popped corn	30 vanilla caramels	2 tbsp. water	1/8 tsp. salt

Melt caramels and water in double boiler (or in glass jar in microwave for 1 minute). Stir until smooth. Put the hot popped corn in a large buttered bowl and sprinkle with the salt. Then pour the melted caramel over the popcorn and toss until well coated. Butter your hands and shape the mixture into 2-inch balls or press into shapes (tree, snowman).
Variation: Use the Caramel Syrup from the above recipe in place of the 30 vanilla caramels.

Chapter Twenty-Three: Sweet Treats

Basic Pudding

| 1.5 tbsp. corn starch | 2 tbsp. granulated sugar | 1 cup cold milk | 1/2 tsp. vanilla extract |

Add the corn starch and the sugar to 1/4 cup cold milk. Scald the rest of the milk in the top of a double boiler. Gradually add the corn starch and sugar mixture while stirring constantly. Continue to cook over low heat for 2 minutes. When the pudding starts to boil, cover the boiler with a lid, and cook on low heat for another 5 minutes. Add the vanilla extract. Remove from heat and chill in the refrigerator.
Variation - Chocolate Pudding: Increase sugar to 3 tbsp. and add 1 tsp. butter and 1.5 tsp. cocoa to the corn starch mixture.

Chocolate Pudding

2/3 cup granulated sugar	1/3 cup corn starch	1/4 tsp. salt
1/3 cup cocoa powder	1.5 tsp. vanilla extract	3 cups milk

Preparation: Combine the sugar, cocoa powder, corn starch, and salt in a bowl and mix well.
Cook: Heat 3 cups of milk over medium heat until bubbles appear around the inside edges of the pot and then remove the pot from the heat. Pour 1/2 cup of the warm milk into the bowl with the dry ingredients and stir to make a smooth paste. Then put the paste into the pot with the rest of the milk. Add the vanilla extract (if available), and stir until well blended. Heat the mixture in the pot over medium heat for about 3 or 4 minutes, stirring constantly, until the mixture thickens to the consistency of pudding. If the pudding starts to bubble, reduce the heat. Pour the pudding into serving bowls and chill.

Kool Aid Pudding (or Pie Glaze)

1 or 2 packages of Kool Aid (any flavor)	2 quarts water
8 tbsp. corn starch	1 cup granulated sugar

Note: Use 1 tablespoon of corn starch per cup of water.
Mix dry ingredients in a large sauce pan. Add water and bring to boil. Stir until thick and clear. Let cool and serve.
Variation - Pie Glaze: Increase corn starch to 10 tbsp. and it makes a good glaze for strawberry or raspberry pie or other fruit.

Pioneer Pudding

1/3 cup cornmeal	1 tsp. ginger	1 tsp. salt
5 cups milk	1/2 cup honey, or molasses, or corn syrup	

Add the cornmeal to the milk and cook in a double boiler for 20 minutes. Add the ginger, salt, and honey. Stir well. Pour into a buttered pan and bake for 2 hours at 250°F.

Chilled Blueberry and Mint Rice Pudding (Serves Four)

1.5 cups **cooked** white rice	1 cup blueberries	1 tbsp. chopped mint
1 cup low fat milk	3 tbsp. sugar	nutmeg (optional garnish)

Combine all, except mint and nutmeg, in a saucepan and cook for 15 to 20 minutes over low heat, stirring frequently. Transfer the pudding to a large bowl and stir in the mint. Chill for a least 1 hour before serving. Spoon into serving bowls and sprinkle nutmeg garnish over pudding.

Chapter Twenty-Three: Sweet Treats

Warm Rice Pudding (Serves Four)

1/2 cup **uncooked** white rice	1/2 tsp. salt	1/2 cup sugar (granulated or brown)
1 quart milk	1/2 tsp. cinnamon	1/2 cup raisins (optional)

Mix all ingredients, except raisins, and pour into a greased baking dish. Bake at 275°F for 3 hours. Stir frequently during the first hour. Add 1/2 cup raisins during the final 30 minutes.

Chilled Rice Sundae (Serves Four)

1/4 cup **ground uncooked** white rice	1 tsp. vanilla extract
3 tbsp. granulated sugar	2.5 cups milk
1/2 tsp. ground cinnamon	berries, or nuts, or chocolate syrup

Combine **ground** white rice, milk, vanilla extract, cinnamon, and sugar in a saucepan. Bring to a boil stirring constantly. Reduce heat and simmer for 30 to 40 minutes, stirring occasionally. (Add a little milk if it begins to dry out.) Allow to cool. When cool, spoon into dessert dishes and chill in the refrigerator. Serve with fresh berries (and/or chopped nuts) (or chocolate syrup) on top.

Homemade Granola

3 cups rolled oats	1/2 cup toasted wheat germ	1 tsp. salt
1 cup shredded coconut	1/2 cup sesame seeds	1/3 cup honey or maple syrup
1/3 cup melted butter	1 cup chopped almonds	1/2 cup raisins

Preparation: Stir everything, except raisins, together. Spread in a 15x10x1 inch baking pan.
Cook: Bake at 375°F for 15 to 20 minutes stirring once. Remove from oven and stir in the raisins. Cool. Store in an air tight container in a cool, dry place or in the refrigerator. Makes about 7 cups.

Chewy Granola Bars (24 Bars)

1/2 cup brown sugar	1/2 cup butter	1/3 cup honey
5 cups homemade granola (above recipe)		1/2 cup wheat flour

Combine brown sugar, butter, and honey in a saucepan and bring to a boil stirring constantly. In a large bowl stir together the granola and the flour. Then pour the brown sugar mixture over the granola mixture and stir until well coated. Press into a 9x13 inch pan. Cool. Cut into bars.

Corn Cob Jelly

12 sweet corn cobs	4 cups water	3.5 tbsp. fruit pectin	4 cups granulated sugar

Put corn cobs in water and bring to a boil and then boil for 10 minutes. Measure 3 cups liquid and strain through a cheesecloth. Put strained liquid into a large saucepan. Add pectin. Bring to rolling boil. Add sugar. Bring mixture back to a boil. Simmer for 3 minutes. Then skim. Add food coloring, if desired. Pour into scalded jars and seal. The jelly will be clear and it will have an apple-honey flavor.

Pear Preserves

16 cups peeled, sliced pears	1 tbsp. lemon juice	4 cups granulated sugar	2 cups water

Simmer all in a large pot over medium heat until the pears are tender and the syrup is thick. The pears will be slightly translucent. Pour into hot sterilized jars to about 1/4 inch from the top of the jar. Finish by processing jars in a hot water bath.

Chapter Twenty-Three: Sweet Treats

Chapter Twenty-Four

Edible Wild Plants

How to Identify Edible Wild Plants

The best method of identifying edible wild plants is by consulting someone where you live who knows which plants are edible and which ones are not.

Plants eaten by rodents, squirrels, raccoons, and rabbits are **usually** safe for humans. However, birds frequently eat foods that are poisonous to humans. Therefore proceed with caution when experimenting with any wild plant.

Don't experiment with any wild plant unless there is enough of it to provide a steady reliable food source.

Do **not** eat any wild plant unless you can positively identify it and you know it is safe. Plants sometimes look the same as a different plant but they are not the same. Some are safe but most plants are **not** safe to eat. Some wild plants are poisonous. Do **not** eat any wild plant unless you can positively identify it and you know it is safe.

Even if a wild plant can be eaten by other people in your group, you may have an adverse reaction to it. The following four step procedure could help you avoid this problem. The following procedure is appropriately used in an unexpected survival situation when starvation is the alternative.

If you have an adverse reaction to any wild plant you should seek professional medical attention immediately.

Four Step Safety Procedure
to Identify Potentially Edible Wild Plants

1. Rub a little of the plant on the inside of your upper left arm. This is a sensitive area but one that should not incapacitate you. Wait 8 hours to see if your skin breaks out in a rash.

2. Rub a little of the plant on the outside of your lips. Wait 8 hours to see if your lips break out.

3. Put a very small quantity of the plant in your mouth, chew it up really good, and then spit it all out. Wait one day to see if you get sick.

4. Try swallowing a little bit of it the next day. Wait one day to see if you get sick.

Berries

Aggregate berries (raspberries, blackberries) are 99% edible. Purple, blue, and black berries are 90% edible. Only 50% of red berries are edible. Avoid green, yellow, and white berries.

Cattails

Stalks: In the spring the young 2 foot stalks can be peeled and the white inner core eaten raw or boiled.
Flower Heads: In late spring the green flower heads can be husked and roasted or boiled.
Pollen: In early summer the yellow pollen heads can be eaten raw or made into flour. Use a stick to knock the pollen powder into a container. Mix with a little water and stir into a thick batter. Form into 3 inch round flat cakes and bake or fry.
Root: The root is always edible and contains starch. It may be peeled and eaten raw, roasted or boiled. If eaten raw, chew and spit out the fibrous part of the root. They can be crushed, dissolved in cold water, drained, dried and made into flour.

Thin Evergreen Needles (Pine, Spruce, etc.) (Vitamin C)

The thin green needles are an excellent source of vitamin C (but no calories). If you eat them year round then you will notice they taste different during the different seasons. Sometimes the taste is neutral and sometimes a little bitter. Regardless of how they taste, they are still an edible food source. Pine needles may be eaten raw or cooked. Or you can boil them in some water to make a broth or tea.

Pine Needle Juice (Vitamin C)

Split the green needles of young pine, fir, or juniper trees. Put in hot water for 2 or 3 minutes. Then cut into tiny pieces, press, and put in cold water for 2 or 3 hours. If the days are sunny then keep the jar in the sun. Filter and sweeten the juice with some sugar before serving.

Yellow, White, or Red Clover (Spring and Summer) (Vitamin E)

All types of clover are edible (vitamin E). Clover can be recognized by its small round flowers and its three small leaves. Clover leaves may be eaten raw or boiled (older leaves are better boiled). The tiny flowers can be boiled to make a tea. The roots can be scraped, washed, and boiled. Red clover should be eaten sparingly and it should **not** be eaten by pregnant women or nursing mothers.

Daisy (Late Spring to Late Summer)

Young white flower **petals** and young **leaves** can be eaten raw in a salad. Remove and discard the bitter yellow center of the flower.

Birch Juice (Maple Syrup Same Principle)

A young birch tree should be drilled 2 inches deep about 2 feet off the ground with a 7/16" drill bit pointed slightly upwards. Put a tube (plastic pipe) in the hole pointing slightly downwards. Place a pot below the end of the tube. Leave it for 48 hours and wait for the juice to slowly drip into the pot. During April and May you can usually get approximately 8 quarts of juice during 48 hours.

Birch Wine: The juice can be mixed with some sugar and yeast and left to ferment. The fermentation process takes about 2 weeks.

Inner Tree Bark

When the sap is rising in the spring, the soft thin white layer of inner tree bark is edible and nutritious (pine, spruce, birch, elm, popular, maple, willow). Strip off some of the outer bark near the base of the tree (or an exposed root) to get to the inner bark. May be eaten raw but it is more digestible if roasted or boiled into a jelly-like mass. Or dry it and grind it into flour

Lamb's Quarters
(also called Pigweed and Goosefoot)

Contains protein, calcium, potassium, iron, vitamins A, B6, C, K, thiamin, riboflavin, niacin, and minerals. It is an annual between 2 to 4 feet tall. Its most important identification characteristic is that it is almost odorless. It tastes similar to spinach or chard. The main **stalk** is edible and it has multiple side branches. The **leaves** are edible and they are green on top and they may have a silver white dusting on the underside. The white dusting can cause tongue irritation in some people. The lower leaves are goosefoot shaped, 1.25 to 2.75 inches long, 1.25 to 2.5 inches wide. The upper leaves are shaped like a long diamond, 1/2 to 2 inches long, 1/4 to 3/4 inches wide. The top leaves taste the best and are the most tender. In the late summer to early fall the tips of the plant form edible tiny greenish white **flower clusters** on spikes. The **seeds** can be toxic and should **not** be eaten.

Preparation: Lamb's Quarters contains oxalic acid which is easily removed by boiling or steaming, and by discarding the water. However, small quantities may be eaten raw. If the leaves and stems are steamed until tender then they will shrink, turn dark green, and cook quickly. Or the leaves may be dried and stored for winter consumption. Or the leaves may be blanched and frozen..

Dandelions (Spring to Autumn)

The French grow **dandelions** the same way Americans grow lettuce in their gardens.

According to the U.S. Department of Agriculture, **dandelions** are more nutritious than broccoli or spinach, contain more cancer-fighting beta-carotene than carrots, and are a rich source of calcium, iron, magnesium, potassium, thiamin, riboflavin, and dietary fiber.

The **stems and flowers** may be eaten raw or cooked. The flowers can be made into wine. The flowers mature into a puff ball of tufted seeds. Dandelion flowers, from which the bitter stem and green parts need to be removed before using, can be dipped in batter and fried to make fritters or boiled for jellies or used in muffins and wines.

The young, tender **leaves** of dandelions may be eaten raw in salads, or as cooked greens, in gravies, or in a variety of baked dishes. Pick the tender leaves before the flowers bud or they will become bitter. Remove the tough center vein from the leaves before eating. Older leaves taste bitter and should be boiled or steamed to improve their taste.

The **roots** are mildly bitter. Wash the roots, add a pinch of baking soda to remove the bitterness, and boil them like a potato. Or you can dry the roots in the sun, crush or grind them, and use them as a substitute for coffee. The root grows very deep and if broken off, it will grow a new plant. Therefore, never harvest the entire root, or replant the lower half of the root near your home. Harvest dandelion roots during the fall and winter months. Cleaned, roasted and ground up, dandelion roots make a coffee-flavor, caffeine-free base for hot or cold beverages.

Dandelion Greens, Raw, Chopped
Nutrition Facts
Serving Size 1 cup (2 ounces or 55.0 g)

	Amount	% RDV
Calories	24.75	1 %
Calories from Fat	3.5	
Total Fat	0.4 g	1 %
Saturated Fat	0.1 g	2 %
Polyunsaturated Fat	0.17 g	
Monounsaturated Fat	0.01 g	
Cholesterol	0.0 mg	0 %
Total Carbohydrate	5.1 g	2 %
Dietary Fiber	1.9 g	8 %
Sugars	2.1 g	
Protein	1.5 g	3 %
Vitamins		
Vitamin A	2712.1 IU	54 %
B1, Thiamin	0.105 mg	7 %
B2, Riboflavin	0.143 mg	8 %
B5, Pantothenic Acid	0.046 mg	<1 %
Vitamin B6	0.138 mg	7 %
Vitamin B12	0.0 mcg	0 %
Vitamin C	19.25 mg	32 %
Vitamin D	0.0 mcg	0 %
Vitamin E	2.635 mg	9 %
Vitamin K	150.5 mcg	214 %
Niacin	0.443 mg	2 %
Lutein	3656.4 mcg	
Carotene, beta	1627.95 mcg	
Carotene, alpha	0.0 mcg	
Minerals		
Calcium, Ca	102.85 mg	10 %
Copper	0.094 mg	5 %
Iron, Fe	1.705 mg	9 %
Magnesium, Mg	19.8 mg	5 %
Manganese, Mn	0.188 mg	5 %
Phosphorus, P	36.3 mg	4 %
Potassium, K	218.35 mg	11 %
Sodium, Na	41.8 mg	2 %
Selenium, Se	0.275 mg	<1 %
Zinc	0.226 mg	2 %
Other		
Ash	0.99 g	
Folate, DFE	14.85 mcg	

Poke Sallet Weed (Harvest in the Spring to Mid-Summer)

Do **not** confuse the word "sallet" for "salad." The traditional use of these two words has been:
1. Sallet (or salet) refers to **cooked** greens.
2. Salad refers to **uncooked** greens.

In the past **Allens** brand foods sold cooked "Poke Salet Greens" in a 14.5 ounce can until the year 2000.

Uncooked raw poke leaves are mildly poisonous and may cause vomiting and diarrhea, both of which can be easily avoided by boiling the leaves before eating them. Also, poke leaves should be picked in the spring or early summer when they are no more than 6 to 8 inches long. After mid-July, the veins in the leaves turn red and the leaves are too mature and contain toxin levels that can be unsafe.

In the spring poke sallet reaches a height of about two feet. At that time the leaves may be harvested and processed by boiling as explained below.

By late summer the plant can be between six to seven feet tall and then the leaves are **too mature** to be used as food.

When the poke leaves on a poke plant begin to show red veins then the poke plant can be broken off at the ground and discarded. If the weather is still warm then the roots in the ground will produce another poke plant that has fresh young new poke leaves.

Poke weed is recognized by its magenta or purple main stalk. The leaves are between 6 inches to 10 inches long and about 2 to 3 inches wide.

The summer **flowers** are small and white or pinkish and they are followed by green berries which turn dark purple when they ripen. Do not eat the flowers, berries, the main purple stalk that supports the plant, or the root. The root is extremely poisonous.

Never eat the poke berries. However, the **berries** may be crushed and their juice used to make a red dye or a red ink. Inside each berry there are between 8 to 13 black seeds. The **seeds** are also poisonous and the seeds should **never** be eaten.

Nutritional Data
8 ounces (1 cup) cooked poke sallet, drained

Category	Amount	% RDV
Calories	33	2 %
Total Carbohydrate	5.1 g	2 %
Dietary Fiber	2.5 g	10 %
Protein	3.8 g	8 %
Vitamins		
Vitamin A	14,355 IU	287 %
B1, Thiamin	0.12 mg	8 %
B2, Riboflavin	0.41 mg	24 %
B3, Niacin	1.82 mg	9 %
B5, Pantothenic Acid	0.06 mg	1 %
Vitamin B12	0 mcg	0 %
Vitamin C	135.3 mg	14 %
Vitamin D	0 mcg	0 %
Vitamin E	1.4 mg	7 %
Vitamin K	178.2 mcg	223 %
Minerals		
Calcium, Ca	87.5 mg	9 %
Copper, Cu	0.21 mg	10 %
Iron, Fe	2.0 mg	11 %
Magnesium, Mg	23.1 mg	6 %
Manganese, Mn	0.55 mg	28 %
Phosphorus, P	54.5 mg	5 %
Potassium, K	303.6 mg	6 %
Selenium, Se	1.49 mg	2 %
Sodium, Na	30.0 mg	1 %
Zinc, Zn	0.31 mg	2 %
Other		
Folate, DFE	14.85 mcg	

Source: https://ndb.nal.usda.gov/ndb/foods/show/3079?manu=&fgcd=&ds=

Young Poke Leaves

During the Great Depression of the 1930s young poke sallet leaves were widely eaten by many southern families on a regular basis. In my opinion boiled young poke leaves have a consistency and taste similar to a mixture of boiled spinach, collard, and turnip greens.

In the early spring, poke sallet reaches a height of about one or two feet. When the entire plant is 12 inches tall (or shorter) and the new leaves are on top of the new shoots and the plant has not yet formed side branches, then the young tender shoots and leaves may be harvested and prepared following the cooking directions below. However, after the plant has started to produce side branches with leaves then the main purple stalk contains poisons and it should not be eaten. However, if the leaves do not contain red veins then the leaves can be harvested and cooked following the directions that appear below.

Young poke leaves are a good source of vitamins and minerals but they must be cooked.

Poke Sallet Cooking Instructions:
Note: If you prefer very tender cooked greens then boil for the maximum times shown below. If you prefer less tenderness and more firmness then boil for the minimum times shown below.
First Boil: Rinse each leaf by itself under clean running water and then cover the leaves with fresh water in a cook pot. Bring the water to a boil and allow the water to boil for ten to fifteen minutes. Drain as much water as possible from the leaves using a colander or a strainer.
Second Boil: Add fresh clean water to the cook pot and bring the water to a boil and boil the leaves for two to five minutes. Drain as much water as possible from the leaves in a strainer.
Third Boil (Optional): Add fresh clean water to the cook pot. Boil the leaves a third time for one minute and then drain off the water.
Serve the tender pokes leaves the same way you would boiled spinach.

Warnings:

1. Do **not** eat mature poke leaves that have visible red veins in the leaf itself. Only pick young poke sallet leaves.
2. Do **not** eat poke leaves until after you have boiled them at least two times (three times is preferred for safety reasons).
3. Do **not** eat poke leaves if you are pregnant or nursing.

Note: Use the same degree of caution with poke sallet leaves as you would with raw pork meat. Raw pork should never be eaten until after it has been thoroughly cooked. After the pork has been cooked well done then it can be safely consumed. The same principle applies to raw poke sallet leaves.

If poke leaves are eaten after the first boil then some of the harmful substances may still be on the leaves because the leaves were in contact with the water and the harmful substances just prior to eating. If the first water is discarded and fresh water is added to the cook pot, and the leaves are boiled again, then the fresh water has a chance to extract any remaining harmful substances that may still be clinging to the leaves. Never eat the leaves until after they have been boiled in clean water at least two times. After two (or three) boilings young poke sallet leaves may be safely consumed..

Introduction to Kudzu

The three parts of the kudzu plant that are edible are:
1. Young leaves and vine tips.
2. Flower blossoms, and
3. Roots.

Look for a kudzu plant that is **not** near a highway where it will be contaminated by dust and automobile exhaust fumes. Also avoid kudzu that has been sprayed with deadly chemicals to control the growth of the invasive plant.

Beware of insects, birds, spiders, and wild animals that frequently live in kudzu patches. Talk loudly when approaching a kudzu patch to give the critters a chance to depart before you arrive.

Bees also love the flower blossoms so do not provoke them. Wear long pants, a long sleeve shirt, shoes, gloves, and a hat when harvesting kudzu.

Avoid poison ivy and poison oak, which resembles kudzu.

Kudzu Leaves and Vine Tips

In the early spring and throughout the growing season, harvest the very end of an established kudzu vine where the new growth is forming small shoots and young leaves (called runners). Only the young leaves and vine tips are tender enough for human consumption. The older leaves and vines are too tough for the human digestive system.

Wash the kudzu thoroughly in cool water. Then soak the kudzu for 20 minutes in some clean cool water with a little salt added. Rinse and drain. Process immediately or store in the refrigerator for 3 to 4 days in an airtight container.

Kudzu leaves have a soft fuzz on them. The fuzz is offensive to most people when eaten raw. The fuzz wilts quickly when cooked. Therefore briefly dip the fresh leaves in some boiling water and then immediately dip in cold water. The fuzz will wilt, the appearance of the leaves will change, but the taste will remain the same.

Kudzu Leaf Recipes

Kudzu leaves and tender vine tips may be boiled like spinach. Boiled kudzu leaves mix well with other cooked greens including spinach and young poke sallet leaves.

Boiled kudzu leaves blend well with cooked rice and many cooked wild meats.

Fresh kudzu leaves may be processed in a pressure cooker following a spinach canning recipe, and stored in canning jars for future consumption.

Kudzu Flower Blossoms

Kudzu blooms from late July through September, depending on the climate and location. The most common species in the United States has magenta and reddish purple flowers that resemble a wisteria. A less common variety has white blossoms.

Kudzu flowers smell like ripe grapes. However, the blossoms do not taste like grapes. They have a unique flavor that is just a little bit sweet.

The flowers are sometimes hidden behind the green leaves. Pick the flowers when they are dry (not covered with the morning dew or rain). You may just pick the flowers but it is usually easier to cut the entire flower raceme of blossoms and then remove the individual flowers later.

Wash the flowers gently but thoroughly in cool water and then drain. They will remain fresh for one day. Or freeze them for future consumption. Kudzu flowers may be eaten plain or as part of a salad or other dish.

Kudzu Flower Tea

Pour a cup of boiling water over 1/4 cup fresh flowers and let it steep for 4 or 5 minutes. Strain and drink.

Kudzu Roots

Kudzu roots are normally harvested in the winter months. Only a kudzu root that was started from a seedling will produce a root that contains a good quantity and quality of starch. Good kudzu starch roots may weigh up to 200 pounds and be as long as 8 feet. The vast majority of kudzu roots are formed when an established vine touches the ground. Most of the roots growing near the surface are not high quality. Most kudzu roots look like tree roots and they are **not** edible.

Kudzu Root Sucker

In a survival situation, any kudzu root between 1/2 to 3/4 inches in diameter can be washed, cut at both ends to a length of about 6 inches, and then all the exterior bark should be scrapped off. The raw root can then be sucked on to gradually remove all its internal nutrients. Only suck the nutrients out of the root. The root is wood. Wood is **not** digestible. Do **not** eat the wood.

Kudzu Root Tea

The thin, tender young roots can be dug up, washed, diced, boiled, and strained to make a tea.

Nutritional Information (8 Ounces of Fresh Kudzu Leaves)

Calories	258	Calcium	34.3 mg
Protein	4.8%	Phosphorous	41.1 mg
Fiber	45.7%	Iron	1.4 mg
Fat	0.2%	Other Vitamins Are Also Present	

Chapter Twenty-Four: Edible Wild Plants

Chapter Twenty-Five

Acorn Information, Identification, Processing, and Recipes

History of the Common Ordinary Acorn

The common, ordinary acorn is one of the ancient foods of mankind. The first mention of acorns for human consumption was by the Greeks over 2,000 years ago. Over the course of human history it has been estimated that people have eaten more acorns than both wheat and rice combined. The acorn has served as an important famine food for many centuries. Acorns may be eaten alone or in a wide variety of acorn recipes.

Native American Indian tribes all across North America, such as the Cherokee, Pima, and Apache, used acorns as one of their primary staple foods in the same way they used corn. American Indians understood the food value of the acorn and how to prepare it for human consumption. Some Indian tribes would bury their acorns in the mud for many days and then dig them up and dry them in the sun. Other Indian tribes would put their acorns inside a reed basket with a few heavy rocks and then put the basket in a fast moving stream for several days. Both of these methods removed the tannin in the acorns and made them fit for people to eat. There is now an easier, more scientific method and it will be described in detail as you continue to read.

Acorn Facts

One tall mature oak tree can produce almost one-thousand pounds of acorns in one growing season during normal weather conditions. Acorns have a low sugar content and therefore help control blood sugar levels. They have a sweet nutty aftertaste. Acorn meal may be used in bread and stew recipes, substituting acorn meal for approximately one-fourth of the flour. Since acorns contain natural sweetness you should reduce any other sweeteners in the recipe by one-fourth. Acorn grits can be used in place of nuts in cookie, brownie, and bread recipes. Acorns are a reliable source of carbohydrates, protein, 6 vitamins, 8 minerals, and 18 amino acids, and they are lower in fat than most other nuts. One handful of acorns is equivalent in nutrition to a pound of fresh hamburger.

Oak Trees

White Oak: White oak trees live between 450 to 650 years (and longer). They can exceed 4 feet in diameter and 100 feet tall. The white oak is the most common species of oak tree. The leaf has a dark green glossy top side and a light green under side. The leaf lobe ends (edges) are rounded. White oak acorns mature in one growing season. Acorn production is heaviest approximately every third year. The inner shell of white oak acorns is smooth and the inner nutmeat is whitish in color. Split one of the inner nutmeats in half and you will see the whitish color. This is why the tree is called a white oak. White oak acorns are low in tannic acid and are naturally sweet and may be eaten with minimal processing. They are the best acorns for use in acorn recipes.

Red Oak: A red oak tree leaf has a glossy green top side and a fuzzy under side. The leaf lobe ends are very pointed. Red oak acorns require two years to mature. Red oak acorns have a hairy lining inside the shell and the nutmeat is yellowish in color. They are very high in tannic acid and therefore taste very bitter. Red oak acorns **must** be processed before eating. Generally red oak acorns are not harvested for human consumption except during serious famine conditions. (Caution: Excessive amounts of tannic acid can lead to kidney failure. Therefore if you must consume red oak acorns then you should process them for the maximum amount of time.)

There are several other varieties of oak trees but the white oak is the most common oak tree throughout the United States, followed by the red oak.

If all the oak trees in your area are exactly the same then they will all produce acorns that taste the same. But if you have different varieties of oaks then you will have different varieties of acorns which will taste different. Therefore, when you harvest your acorns, keep the ones you collect under each oak tree in a separate bag or container by themselves until you do a taste test to determine if any have a more agreeable taste than the others. If so, note which tree(s) they came from, and focus your next year's collection efforts there. You **must** harvest your acorns **very soon** after they fall to the ground or the squirrels, deer, and other wildlife will eat them. If the acorns stay on the ground very long, they will become infested with insect larva, and they will also absorb ground moisture and begin to mold.

Acorn Collection

Collect your acorns every day from September through October as soon as possible after they have fallen off the oak tree onto the ground. They may be green, or green and tan, or brown. The green ones aren't fully ripe yet but collect them also because they will ripen to a dark brown in a few more days. In my opinion the green ones are better because they have just fallen off the tree and therefore they have had less time to absorb ground moisture or be attacked by insects. If you happen to notice that an acorn is defective when you pick it up then toss it into the woods where there are no oak trees. Otherwise there is a good chance you will be picking up that same acorn every day for many weeks to come.

After collecting all the acorns you can find each day, sit down and go through your new batch of acorns. Remove and discard the cap or crown of the acorn. Inspect the acorns (first inspection) and discard any that have an obvious defect, or signs of mold, or a tiny hole because it probably contains a worm. The acorns should feel firm between your fingers. Discard any that are soft.

Acorn Drying Methods

Spread the good acorns you collect each day onto a tray, board, or screen. You can then dry the acorns using any one of following three methods:

1. house drying at normal room temperatures, or
2. the sun, or
3. a conventional oven.

House Drying at Normal Room Temperatures: Allow the acorns to dry gradually inside your home at normal room temperatures. The acorns should only be one layer thick on the drying trays. If the acorns are relatively green then this drying method normally takes between two to four weeks.

The advantages of room temperature drying are:

1. The inner acorn nutmeat retains most of its original moisture which adds to its flavor and chewability.
2. If your home is free of flying insects then you will not loose any more acorns to insect larva.

The disadvantages of room temperature drying are:

1. It can take as long as four weeks to properly dry the acorns.
2. Each day you will need **more** house space to dry additional acorns.
3. Periodically you will have to inspect your acorns for tiny worms.
4. Future acorn nutmeat mold problems are more likely to occur.

Sun Drying: Place the tray of acorns in direct sunlight for two to five consecutive days, depending on how "green" your acorns are when you collect them. Bring all your acorns inside each night. Drying in the sun is the traditional method. If the sky is partly cloudy or overcast then you may need to dry your acorns for more than five days in the sun. (Note: If your acorns are not completely dry then they will soon be covered with mold and you will have to throw them away. Any acorns that are still partially green after a few days of drying should be separated from the rest of the acorns. Continue drying any partially green acorns until they turn completely brown.)

The advantages of sun drying are:

1. It helps to kill insect larva.
2. It helps to reduce future mold problems.

The disadvantages of sun drying are:

1. Flying insects will lay eggs in some of the acorns and they will have to be thrown away.
2. The inner nutmeat looses some of its moisture and flavor.
3. The shelf life of the nutmeat is between four to six months.

If you have windows facing the sun then you can place your tray of acorns in the sun inside your house and eliminate the flying insect problem.

Oven Drying: Place the tray of acorns in a warm oven (175ºF) for about 20 minutes with the oven door slightly cracked to let the moisture escape.

The advantages of oven drying are:

1. Drying can be done very quickly.
2. It effectively kills all insect larva.
3. It eliminates future mold problems.

The disadvantages of oven drying are:

1. The inner nutmeat looses most of its moisture and flavor and it becomes very hard to chew.
2. The shelf life of the nutmeat is only two or three months.

Of the above three different drying methods, I prefer sun drying inside my home in front of a window that faces the sun.

Acorn Storage

After drying your acorns, inspect them again (second inspection). The drying process helps to reveal cracks or insect holes you couldn't see when the acorns were still damp. Discard any acorns that don't have a good exterior shell, or process and use those acorns immediately. Acorns with a cracked outer shell will dry out quickly on the inside and the nutmeat will be lost.

It is also possible that small flying insects may have laid eggs inside some of your acorns while they were drying in the sun, if they could find a convenient entrance to the nutmeat area, such as a crack or hole or other imperfection. Those eggs will hatch in a short time and you will be able to identify the bad acorns when they do (they will have a small hole in them).

If you discover tiny holes in your acorns after they have dried then discard the bad acorns and place the acorns without any holes on a cookie sheet and dry them in a warm oven at 175ºF for 15 minutes with the oven door slightly cracked to let the moisture escape. The heat will kill any remaining insect larva inside the acorns.

Approximately one-week later, inspect your dried acorns for the third time and look for mold or worms or other major problems. Discard any acorns with mold (or process and use them immediately), or the mold will soon spread throughout your entire batch.

Approximately one-week later, inspect your dried acorns for the fourth time. Remove and discard any defective or moldy acorns (or process and use them immediately).

If you discover mold on your acorns at this point then they were not thoroughly dry at the beginning. If the mold is not severe then place the batch of acorns on a cookie sheet and dry them in a warm oven at 175ºF for 15 minutes with the oven door slightly cracked to let the moisture escape and to kill the mold.

You may now store your thoroughly inspected, dried acorns in a cool, dry place until you need them. Store your acorns in several different containers. (Note: Zipper freezer bags work extremely well for storing acorns.) If the acorns in one container become unusable then your other acorns should still be okay. Properly dried and stored, acorns still in their original shell will remain edible for several months.

As time passes the inner acorn nutmeat gradually dries out and loses most of its flavor and it becomes too hard too chew. Therefore you should process and eat your acorns as soon as practical after collecting them. The longer they are stored, the more they will continue to dry out and become unfit for human consumption. **Even under the best storage conditions at room temperature, most acorns will not be edible after six-months of storage.**

If you have freezer storage space available then you may remove the acorn nutmeats from their exterior shell and freeze only the nutmeats inside a zipper freezer bag. This will help to preserve the moisture content of the nutmeats and significantly extend their shelf life and flavor.

Acorn Preparation

Acorns must be processed before they can be used in acorn recipes.

Do **not** remove your acorn nutmeats from their protective outer shell until you are ready to process and eat them. The inner acorn nutmeat kernels will dry up and shrivel after a few days of exposure to the air. The inner white nutmeat will gradually darken and it will begin to dry out the longer it is exposed to the air.

First crack the thin outer shell of the acorn. It will crack easily with an ordinary nut cracker, or pliers, or by squeezing firmly with your thumb and forefinger. Only crack the shell. Peel off the shell and save the inner nutmeat kernel for future processing. Sometimes you will split the inner acorn nutmeat in half as you crack the outer shell. That is okay. You may taste one acorn nutmeat kernel from each batch of acorns to determine if one of your local trees produces sweeter acorns than the other trees. After chewing and tasting, you should spit it out.

Our bodies are all different and we can not all eat the same foods as everyone else. For example, some people are allergic to milk and milk products. It is always a good idea to eat a very small amount of any new food that you have never eaten before to determine whether or not your body will have an adverse reaction to it. Therefore if you have never eaten acorn nutmeats before then you should only eat **one** and see how your body reacts. If you are allergic to other nuts then you will probably not be able to eat acorn nutmeats. And you should **not** eat and swallow an acorn nutmeat until **after** you have removed the tannic acid from the acorn nutmeats.

Tannic Acid

All acorns contain tannic acid (or tannin). White Oak acorns contain very little but Red Oak acorns contain a lot. The good news is that tannic acid is water soluble and it can be easily leeched out of the acorns using either:

1. boiling, or
2. cold water flushing.

Too much boiling will result in a loss of nut flavor and it will change the consistency of the nutmeats into a gooey mess.

There are also two ways to process the acorn nutmeats:

1. as whole nutmeat kernels, or
2. as ground nutmeats.

Whole Nutmeat Kernels

If your original taste test of the raw unprocessed acorn nutmeats revealed little or no noticeable bitterness then you may process your nutmeats as whole kernels. This preserves the appearance of the nut and it is useful because some recipes specify whole nuts. It also makes eating the nuts as a snack much easier.

Ground Nutmeats

If your original taste test of the raw unprocessed acorn nutmeats revealed an unpleasant degree of bitterness, then grinding the nutmeats is necessary because it allows the tannic acid to be removed with minimum boiling or flushing. Begin with whole acorn nutmeat kernels (without the cap and without the shell). Crush or grind the acorn nutmeats into smaller pieces or into a coarse meal using a hand grinder, or a flat rock, or a blender. If you use a blender then add a little water to make a liquid mush.

Boiling Method (Removes Tannic Acid)
(May be used with whole nutmeat kernels or ground nutmeats.)

Fill two pots with clean fresh water. Each pot should contain enough water to completely cover the acorn nutmeats (but don't add the nutmeats yet). Turn on the heat to the first pot of water. Taste one of the unprocessed nutmeats to determine the degree of bitterness it contains before boiling.

Note: Add pickling or canning salt to the final pot of boiling water before adding the nutmeats. The salt enhances the flavor of the nutmeats and it also increases their storage life.

Note: It is **not** uncommon for many white oak acorns to contain little or no noticeable bitterness. However, we are not all gifted with the same degree of sensitivity in our taste buds. What may taste pleasant to you may taste slightly bitter to someone else. And regardless of how they taste, all acorns contain some tannic acid. Therefore you should boil all acorn nutmeats at least **one** time. But you may stop after one boiling if your original taste test revealed little or no bitterness in the original unprocessed acorn nutmeats. If you are only going to boil one time you will not need the second pot and you should add the salt to the first pot of boiling water **before** you add the nutmeats.

First Boil: When the first pot starts to boil, add the acorn nutmeats to the first pot of boiling water and immediately **turn off the heat** to the first pot. Turn on the heat to the second pot to start the water in the second pot boiling. Wait 30 minutes and the water in the first pot will be brown. Pour the acorns and the brown water through a strainer or coffee filter to separate the nutmeats from the brown water.

If there was no noticeable bitterness to begin with and you are only using one boil then skip down to the drying instructions below.

Taste one of the nutmeats. If the bitterness is almost gone then you will not need a third boiling and you should add the salt to the second pot of boiling water.

Note: Save the brown water from the first boiling for one of the uses suggested later in this chapter.

Second Boil: Put the nutmeats into the second pot of boiling water and immediately **turn off the heat.** Rinse the first pot and fill with fresh water for the third boiling. Wait 30 minutes. Strain the nutmeats from the brown water in the second pot. (Discard the brown water unless you want to keep it for another purpose.) Taste one nutmeat. If the bitterness is gone then skip to the drying instructions below. If the bitterness is almost gone then add the salt to the third boiling. However, if the bitterness is still unpleasant then wait until the fourth boiling to add the salt.

Third Boil: Follow instructions for second boil. Then taste one nutmeat. The original bitterness should be gone and it should have a sweet, nutlike flavor. (If the nutmeats should fail your taste test at this point then boil a fourth time.)

Dry the nutmeats following the drying instructions below.

Note 1: If you switch the nutmeats from boiling water into cool water and then bring the water to a boil, you will lock in the bitterness and you won't be able to get it out.

Note 2: Do **not** let wet nutmeats sit for hours between boilings. The nutmeats will mold if you do.

Cold Water Flushing Method (Removes Tannic Acid)
(May be used with whole nutmeat kernels or ground nutmeats with very little initial bitterness.)

Cold water flushing is only appropriate for acorns with little initial bitterness. Put the acorn nutmeats inside a clean pillowcase and leech in cold running water (faucet or stream) for several hours until the bitter taste is gone. Periodically squeeze as much water out of the pillowcase and acorn nutmeats as you can without damaging the nutmeats. Then continue rinsing. When the nutmeats no longer taste bitter then you can stop rinsing. Then dry the nutmeats following the drying instructions below.

Uses for the Brown Acorn Water

Save the brown water from the first boiling (discussed above). The brown water should be stored in the refrigerator. With the passage of time a mold will form on top of the water and you will need to boil the water again to kill the mold. Then refrigerate the water again until needed. The brown water may be used in any of the following ways:

Laundry Detergent: Two cups of the brown water can be used as laundry detergent for one load of clothes. Your clothes will smell very good but lighter colors (and whites) will take on a tan tint.

Traditional Herbal Home Remedies: The brown water has both antiseptic and antiviral properties.

1. It can be used to wash the skin to ease the discomfort of skin rashes, burns, and small cuts.
2. It can be used externally to help treat hemorrhoids.
3. Pour some of the water into ice cube trays and freeze it. Then rub it on poison ivy blisters. It soothes and heals the blisters and helps reduce the itching. It is very effective on about 95% of the people who try it and the poison ivy is cured in three days. The cold ice also helps to soothe the inflamed tissues.

Hide Tanning: The brown water can be used in the process of animal hide tanning. Just soak the clean, scraped animal hides in the water. The reason the bitter ingredient in acorns is called "tannic acid" is because it was originally used to tan animal hides.

Drying

If you need the damp acorn nutmeats in a bread recipe then you may use them immediately without drying. However, if you are not going to use the nutmeats until later then you **must** dry them.

After removing the tannin using either boiling or flushing, spread the damp nutmeats in a thin layer on a baking tray and dry slowly in a warm oven (175°F to 200°F) with the door slightly cracked to let the moisture escape. Or place the tray of damp nutmeats in the sun near a window. (If you dry them outside in the sun then cover them with a clean screen or the wildlife will steal them.)

If you are drying ground nutmeats then the dried meal will be caked and it will need to be ground again.

If you are drying whole nutmeat kernels then you may eat them like nuts. Or you may use them in recipes that use whole nuts. Or you may process some of them into grits or meal on an as-needed basis.

Acorn Grits

Follow the tannin removal and drying instructions for acorn nutmeats above. Then pound or grind into course meal or grits. Acorn grits may be used in acorn recipes in place of chopped nuts.

Acorn Meal (or Acorn Flour)

Follow above Grits recipe but grind the acorns into a fine meal.

Storage of Acorn Grits or Acorn Meal

Store in a sealed, glass jar in a cool, dark place. They will keep for several weeks in the refrigerator or for several months in the freezer. Frozen nutmeats will retain their original flavor for about 10 months (or until the next crop of acorns is ready to be harvested). Because they contain nut oil, they will go rancid if left in a warm environment after they have been processed.

Caution: If stored for a very long time then smell them before using. If a musty smell is present then throw them away.

Grandpappy's Basic Acorn Recipes

1. **If you don't like the taste of dried acorns then none of these recipes will appeal to you.**
2. Acorn grits may be deep fried and eaten as a side dish.
3. Acorn grits may be added to soups or salads.
4. Acorn grits may be fried briefly in a skillet and then used as one of the ingredients in a granola snack recipe.
5. Acorn meal may be used in most recipes to replace 1/4 of the flour or 1/4 of the corn meal. However, since acorn meal contains natural sweetness you should reduce any other sweeteners in the recipe by 1/4.
6. 100% Acorn Bread will be hard if baked too long and crumbly if not baked long enough.
7. Ground acorn nutmeats may be roasted and then used as a weak coffee substitute.

Indian Acorn Griddlecakes

| 2 cups acorn meal | 3/4 cup water | 1/2 tsp. salt |

Preparation: Combine everything and beat to a stiff batter. Let stand for one hour.
Cook: Heat 1 tbsp. of fat or oil in frying pan. Drop batter into pan to form cakes about 3 to 4 inches across. Brown cakes slowly on both sides. These cakes will keep for several days.

Mexican Acorn Tortillas

| 2 cups acorn meal | 3/4 cup flour | 2 tsp. salt |

Preparation: Mix ingredients. Add just enough water to make a stiff dough. Let stand for 30 minutes.
Cook: Squeeze into small balls and then press each ball into a very thin flat cake. Fry in a lightly greased skillet until brown on both sides. Use just enough fat or oil to prevent sticking.

Acorn Pemmican Tortillas

| 1/2 cup acorn meal | 1 pound lean meat, cut in thin strips | Several tortillas |

Cook: Boil the lean meat in salted water until tender. Drain and allow to dry. Grind the meat and the acorn meal together using a fine grinding blade. Mix well and then grind a second time. Heat and serve wrapped in a tortilla, or on any flat bread.
Variation: Add cooked white rice, or cooked beans, or hot sauce, or grated cheese as part of the tortilla stuffing.

Pioneer Acorn Bread and Acorn Muffins

1 cup acorn meal	1 cup flour	1 tsp. salt
3 tbsp. baking powder	3 tbsp. oil	1 cup milk (or water)

Optional: You may add 1 egg to the above ingredients.
Preparation: Combine milk, egg (if available), and oil and beat until smooth. Mix in the acorn meal, flour, salt, and baking powder and stir into a smooth dough. Place in a greased bread pan.
Cook: Bake at 400°F for 30 minutes. Cool and serve.
Variation - Acorn Muffins: Fill greased muffin tins about 2/3 full with the above mixture and bake at 400°F for 20 minutes.

Pioneer Acorn Pancakes

Preparation: Use the above recipe for Pioneer Acorn Bread, but use 2 eggs and 1.25 cups milk.
Cook: Drop batter from a ladle onto a hot greased grill. When bottom is brown, turn once and brown other side. Serve with butter, or syrup, or honey, or jelly, or fresh fruit.

Breakfast Acornmeal (Similar to Oatmeal)

1 cup acorn meal	2.5 cups water	1 tsp. salt
1 tsp. honey or sugar	1/8 cup hickory nuts or black walnuts, crushed	

Boil the water with the salt. Add the acorn meal and continue boiling for 15 minutes. Turn off heat. Allow to cool for about five minutes. Stir in the honey and nuts.

Acorn and Corn Meal Mush

1/2 cup acorn meal	4 cups water	1 cup corn meal	1 tsp. salt

Cook: Bring 4 cups of water to a boil in the top half of a double boiler. Add the salt. Sprinkle the acorn meal slowly into the boiling water and stir continuously. Then add the corn meal. When the mixture starts to bubble, it should be able to support a plastic or wooden stirring spoon in the center without the spoon falling over. If too thick, add a little water. If too thin, add a little more cornmeal. Then put the mixture which is in the top half of the double boiler into the bottom half of the double boiler that contains boiling water. Simmer about 45 minutes, stirring occasionally to break up any lumps, until the mush becomes thick. Serve hot for breakfast, lunch, or supper.
Variation: May be served with a topping of milk, or butter, or grated cheese, or bacon bits, or honey, or sugar, or fruit, or jam.
Variation: Pour above finished, cooked mush into a greased loaf pan and put in the refrigerator for about 8 hours. It will become solid and then it can be sliced with a knife into 1/2 inch thick slices. Coat each slice with flour and fry in a very thin layer of oil, one side at a time. Serve with butter, or syrup, or jam (similar to French toast).

Acorn Bread

2 cups acorn meal	1/2 cup milk (or water)	1 tbsp. baking powder
2 cups wheat flour	3 tbsp. butter or olive oil	1 egg (optional)

Optional Sweeteners: Add 1/3 cup honey or maple syrup or sugar, if available.
Preparation: Combine all the above ingredients and pour into a loaf pan.
Cook: Bake at 400°F for 30 minutes or until done. Yields a moist bread with a sweet nutty flavor.

Glazed Acorn Treats

Boiled dry whole acorn kernels	2 cups sugar	1/2 tsp. salt
1/8 tsp. cream of tartar	1 cup water	

Preparation: Mix and dissolve the sugar, salt, and cream of tartar in 1 cup of water.
Cook: Bring above mixture to a boil in a small pot. Continue to boil until the mixture first begins to show signs of browning. Then immediately put the small pot into a larger pot of boiling water to keep the mixture in a liquid state. (Or use a double boiler.) Use a pair of tweezers to dip individual whole acorn kernels (previously shelled, boiled and dried), one at a time into the mixture and then put each acorn onto a sheet of wax paper to dry and harden. Serve as a candied covered nut.

Acorn Cookies

2 cups wheat flour	1 cup white (or brown) sugar	1 tsp. salt
1 cup acorn grits	1/2 cup shortening	1 tsp. baking powder (or baking soda)

Preparation: Combine the flour, baking powder, and salt. In a large bowl, cream the shortening and the sugar. Gradually blend in the dry ingredients. Then blend in the acorn grits. Pinch off walnut sized pieces of dough and roll into balls. Place 1.5" apart on a lightly greased baking sheet.
Cook: Bake at 350°F for 10 to 12 minutes or until lightly colored. Transfer to a wire rack to cool.
Variation: Add 1 egg and/or 1 tsp. vanilla extract.

Acorns, Shelled, Dried
Actual Lab Analysis Results Vary for Different Acorn Varieties and from One Growing Season to the Next

Nutrition Facts
Serving Size: 1 ounce (28.4 g)
Minimum and Maximum values shown below

Category	Amount	% RDV
Calories	109.7 to 144.5	7 %
Calories from Fat	60.9 to 80.3	
Total Fat	6.8 to 8.9 g	14 %
Saturated Fat	0.9 to 1.2 g	45 %
Polyunsaturated Fat	1.3 to 1.7 g	
Monounsaturated Fat	4.3 to 5.7 g	
Cholesterol	0.0 mg	0 %
Total Carbohydrate	11.55 to 15.2 g	5 %
Protein	1.74 to 2.3 g	5 %

Vitamins

Vitamin A	11.06 to 11.14 IU	Less 1 %
B1, Thiamin	0.03 to 0.042 mg	3 %
B2, Riboflavin	0.03 to 0.044 mg	3 %
B3, Niacin	0.52 to 0.683 mg	3 %
B5, Pantothenic Acid	0.20 to 0.267 mg	3 %
Vitamin B6	0.15 to 0.197 mg	10 %
Vitamin B12	0.0 mcg	0 %
Vitamin C	0.0 mcg	0 %
Vitamin D	0.0 mcg	0 %
Vitamin E	0.0 mcg	0 %

Minerals

Calcium, Ca	11.62 to 15.34 mg	2 %
Copper, Cu	0.18 to 0.23 mg	12 %
Iron, Fe	0.22 to 0.29 mg	2 %
Magnesium, Mg	17.58 to 23.29 mg	6 %
Manganese, Mn	0.38 to 0.39 mg	10 %
Phosphorus, P	22.40 to 29.25 mg	3 %
Potassium, K	152.81 to 201.36 mg	10 %
Sodium, Na	0.0 mg	0 %
Zinc, Zn	0.15 to 0.19 mg	1 %

Amino Acids

Alanine	0.100 to 0.131 g
Arginine	0.135 to 0.177 g
Aspartic Acid	0.181 to 0.238 g
Cystine	0.031 to 0.041 g
Glutamic Acid	0.282 to 0.369 g
Glycine	0.081 to 0.107 g
Histidine	0.049 to 0.064 g
Isoleucine	0.081 to 0.107 g
Leucine	0.140 to 0.183 g
Lysine	0.110 to 0.143 g
Methionine	0.029 to 0.039 g
Phenylalanine	0.077 to 0.101 g
Proline	0.070 to 0.092 g
Serine	0.075 to 0.098 g
Thyptophan	0.021 to 0.028 g
Threonine	0.067 to 0.089 g
Tyrosine	0.053 to 0.070 g
Valine	0.099 to 0.129 g

Other

Ash	0.386 to 0.506 mg
Folate, DFE	24.66 to 32.66 mcg

Chapter Twenty-Six

Hickory Nut Recipes

Hickory Nuts (Same Tree Family as Walnuts and Pecans)

Hickory trees grow wild in many areas and they can live for 300 to 500 years. The male and female flowers grow on the same tree. Some hickory nuts are very hard to crack and others are not. Some hickory nuts are delicious but some hickory nuts are bitter and they are only eaten by wildlife, such as squirrels. Sweet tasting hickory nuts may be substituted in almost any recipe in place of pecans or walnuts.

Mother Marsh's Hickory Nut Cake
From "Merry Christmas Cakes," by Marilyn Kluger,
The Courier-Journal, 11/17/1993, Louisville, KY, Pp. E1, E4
This cake was sent to Margaret Mitchell (Gone With the Wind)
every Christmas since 1936 by her Mother-in-Law

1/2 lb. butter	1 tbsp. baking powder	1.5 lbs. seedless raisins
2 cups sugar	1 tbsp. ground cinnamon	1 lb. currants
4 cups flour	2.5 tsp. ground nutmeg	1/2 cup milk
6 eggs	2 cups hickory nut kernels	Optional: 1/2 cup Kentucky Bourbon

Preparation: Grease and flour one large bundt cake pan or two large loaf pans (10"x5"x3") and line with wax paper. Preheat oven to 300°F. Cream the butter and sugar together until fluffy. Beat in the eggs, one at a time, and continue beating until well blended. Stir in the flour, baking powder, nutmeg, and cinnamon. (Reserve a small amount of flour mixture to toss with nuts and fruits before adding them to the batter.) Add the flour mixture and milk alternately to the creamed mixture, in about 3 additions. Then gently stir in the floured fruits and nuts. Scrape batter into prepared pans.
Cook: Bake at 300°F for 3.5 hours if using the bundt pan, or 2 to 2.5 hours in the two loaf pans. Insert a toothpick into the center of the cake to verify doneness (it should be dry when removed). Cook cake on a wire rack. Wrap cake in aluminum foil and store in the refrigerator.
Optional: If desired, wrap cake in a cheesecloth that has been soaked in bourbon. This option was added by Mother Marsh's brother, Bob, one Christmas when he baked the cakes instead of Mother Marsh, his sister.

Hickory Nut Pie

1 cup chopped hickory nuts	3 eggs, slightly beaten	2 tbsp. soft butter
1 cup white Karo corn syrup	3/4 cup granulated sugar	1 tsp. vanilla extract

You will also need one unbaked pie shell.
Preparation: Mix the eggs, sugar, syrup, vanilla, and butter. Then add the nuts. Pour into a pie shell.
Cook: Bake at 400°F for 10 minutes and then reduce heat to 350°F and bake for another 40 minutes.
Variation: Substitute 1 cup of dark brown sugar for white sugar and increase butter to 6 tbsp. Bake at 350°F for 40-45 minutes.

Hickory Nuts Nutritional Information

Nutrition Facts
Hickory Nuts, Shelled, Meat Only
Serving Size: 1 ounce (28.4 g) or 9 Nuts

Category	Amount	% RDV
Calories	187.7	9 %
Total Fat	18.2 g	29 %
Monounsaturated	9.32 g	
Polyunsaturated	6.25 g	
Total Carbohydrate	5.2 g	2 %
Dietary Fiber	1.8 g	8 %
Protein	3.6 g	8 %
Vitamins		
Vitamin A	37.43 IU	Less 1%
B1, Thiamin	0.25 mg	17 %
B2, Riboflavin	0.04 mg	3 %
B3, Niacin	0.26 mg	3 %
B5, Pantothenic Acid	0.49 mg	5 %
Vitamin B	60.05 mg	2 %
Vitamin B12	0 mcg	0 %
Vitamin C	0.57 mcg	1 %
Vitamin D	0 mcg	0 %
Vitamin E	0 mcg	0 %
Minerals		
Calcium, Ca	17.3 mg	2 %
Copper, Cu	0.2 mg	11 %
Iron, Fe	0.6 mg	3 %
Magnesium, Mg	48.9 mg	13 %
Manganese, Mn	1.3 mg	35 %
Phosphorus, P	95.1 mg	10 %
Potassium, K	123.4 mg	6 %
Selenium, Se	2.3 mg	4 %
Sodium, Na	0.3 mg	Less 1%
Zinc, Zn	1.2 mg	11 %

Amino Acids	
Alanine	0.189 g
Arginine	0.596 g
Cystine	0.077 g
Glutamic Acid	0.824 g
Glycine	0.202 g
Histidine	0.111 g
Isoleucine	0.165 g
Leucine	0.293 g
Lysine	0.142 g
Methionine	0.086 g
Phenylalanine	0.204 g
Proline	0.163 g
Serine	0.230 g
Tryptophan	0.040 g
Threonine	0.121 g
Tyrosine	0.130 g
Valine	0.209 g
Other	
Ash	0.57 g
Folate, DFE	11.43 mcg

Chapter Twenty-Seven

Fish

Fish: Cut a gash in the underside of the fish from the anal opening to the head. Cut the throat where attached and remove and bury all the entails. Rinse fish to get rid of any blood clots. Wipe inside with a clean cloth. Cook approximately 10 minutes per inch measured at the thickest part. Firm flesh fish can be grilled but soft flesh fish should be baked or fried. If fried, skin and bone the fish first.

Trout: Rub the outside with fat or oil. Salt and pepper the inside to taste. Grill 4 to 6 inches over hot coals for 10 to 12 minutes turning carefully 3 or 4 times with a spatula. The fish will darken and blister in spots but it will stay moist on the inside.

Fried Fish: Cut large fish into 1 inch slices or fillets. Dip in water and then coat in flour. Add salt and pepper. Place in hot frying pan containing 1/8 inch melted fat, oil, or shortening. Brown one side, then turn and brown the other side, allowing 4 to 6 minutes cooking time per side depending on thickness of fish.

Chapter Twenty-Eight

Aquatic and Land Creatures

Frogs: Cut off and keep only the hind legs. Wash in cold water. Turn skin down and strip off skin like a glove. Boil and eat the legs. (Or cover the legs with boiling water and then drain quickly. Shake legs in flour, salt, and pepper in a plastic baggie. Let stand 15 minutes. Fry in hot oil for 3 minutes until brown.) (The leg glands of some frogs cause diarrhea.)

Turtles: Boil until the shell comes off. The meat is then cut up and used to make a soup using any edible plants available. (Note: Older turtles have tougher meat and they should be boiled longer to tenderize the meat before eating.)

Crayfish: Drop live crayfish into boiling water as soon as possible after catching. They spoil very quickly.

Garden Snails: Some snails are edible. However, most wild snails cannot be eaten because they can carry parasites and those parasites can be fatal to humans.

Snakes: Very few snakes are poisonous but all snakes should be treated with respect. A head shot with a 22-bullet or snake-shot is usually adequate. Or hit the snake on the head with a rock or a 6-foot pole to stun and kill it. Cautiously cut off and bury the head of all snakes. If the poison of a dead snake gets into a cut or scrape it can make you sick. Cut the belly of the snake from where its head was towards its tail. Use your finger to strip out the entails as a single piece. Strip off the outer skin by pulling from the top towards the tail. Wash the remaining meat in clean water. Snake may be broiled or grilled whole (or diced and boiled). Or cut into 3 inch pieces, dip in milk or water, roll in flour and/or corn meal, add salt and pepper, and deep fry in hot oil.

Bugs (Emergency Survival Situation ONLY): The following bugs are edible: ants, grubs, slugs, and earthworms. They may be eaten raw (but not alive) or cooked. Nobody I know likes them raw, so the best solution is to dice them into small pieces and cook them in a soup with some other type of wild food. Grasshoppers can also be eaten if you first remove the legs. The legs contain tiny barbs that can get caught in your throat. Don't eat grasshoppers raw because they occasionally contain tiny parasites (which will be killed if you boil the grasshoppers in water). **Never** eat flies, ticks, mosquitoes, centipedes, or spiders.

Chapter Twenty-Nine

Wild Game Recipes

A wise person will **not** form an opinion about the taste of a specific type of wild animal until **after** he or she has had an opportunity to actually eat some of it after the meat has been properly prepared following a traditional recipe. Each of us has different taste preferences and you may discover that some of the following wild game recipes are actually quite delightful.

General Instructions for Processing Wild Game

1. **Always** wear gloves (latex or rubber) when processing wild game. Wild animals may be caring diseases such as trichinosis, or tularemia, or salmonella, and the gloves will protect you from these **potential** diseases while handling the dead animals. If the meat is **thoroughly cooked** then it can be safely eaten even if these diseases **may** have been present in the raw meat.

2. Process the dead animal as soon as possible after it has been slain:
    a. Drain off all the blood by cutting the left jugular neck vein, or cut off and remove the animal's head. Hang small animals upside down by their hind legs, or arrange larger animals so they are facing downhill on a slope.
    b. Carefully remove all the internal organs without spilling their contents on the meat. Discard all the internal organs (except the ones you know are edible).
    c. Most smaller animals (groundhog, opossum, porcupine, raccoon, squirrel) have glands that are located in their small of the back and under each foreleg. Locate, remove and discard those glands. (Note: Groundhogs have seven or eight of these small glands.)
    d. Skin the animal and remove all the fat. The fat will turn rancid very quickly and it must be discarded (or it should be processed immediately).
    e. Do not let the exterior hair or fur of the animal touch its inner meat as it may transmit an undesirable flavor to the meat. If any loose animal hair accidentally falls on the meat then remove and discard the hair immediately.
    f. If the animal was shot then remove and discard any bullet damaged meat and dried blood from the bullet wound area.

3. Clean and cool the meat as quickly as you can. Plastic zipper freezer bags may be filled with ice, snow, or cold creek water. The meat of small animals may be placed between the sealed bags. Or the sealed bags may be placed inside the body cavity of larger animals. If no cooling bags are available then prop open the body cavity of larger animals with some sticks.

4. The meat of wild animals should be **well cooked** to make it is safe for human consumption (similar to pork).
    a. Small animals (such as rabbit or muskrat) may be processed in a manner similar to chicken.
    b. Large animals (such as deer or bear) may be processed in a manner similar to beef.

Additional Processing Instructions for Small Game Animals

Armadillo - (The size of a large house cat.) - Break the outer shell of the armadillo and only remove the edible back meat. Remove and discard any fat clinging to the back meat. Wash in cool water. Then place the back meat in a pot of cool water and allow it to soak for 12 hours inside the refrigerator. Drain and dry. Cut into bite size pieces and dip in oil. Place the meat onto meat skewers and broil slowly over the heat of a campfire.

Beaver - (35 to 65 pounds, 3 to 4 feet long, flat tail) - Carefully remove the two musk glands that are located under the skin in front of the genital area. Hang the gutted beaver in a cool dry area for two days. Place the meat in a covered pot of salted cold water with a vented lid and simmer for 60 minutes. The steam should be allowed to escape through the vent in the pot lid. (If necessary, add more water during the simmering process.) Cut the meat into steak size slices and cook in a skillet containing 1/2 inch of water over low heat. Turn the steaks over frequently so each side cooks slowly. Continue to cook until they are well done.

Beaver Tail - Position the tail over the flames of a campfire until the skin blisters. Remove the tail from the heat and allow it to cool. Then peel off the tail skin. The beaver tail may now be roasted over campfire coals, or it may be simmered in a skillet containing 1/2 inch of water until it is tender.

Groundhog, also called a Woodchuck - (10 to 20 pounds, 2 feet long) - Hang the gutted groundhog in a cool dry area for two days. Then place it in a pot of salted water and allow to soak for 12 hours inside the refrigerator. Drain. The groundhog meat may now be used in a recipe in place of chicken. For example, cut-up groundhog pieces may be coated with salt, pepper, and flour, and then fried in a skillet like chicken.

Muskrat - (2 to 3 pounds, 10 inches long) - Only the hams and shoulders of the muskrat are edible. Remove and discard the musk glands located below the stomach and legs, along with the white stringy meat attached to the musk glands. Place the hams and shoulders in a covered pot of salted cold water with a vented lid and simmer for 45 minutes. The steam should be allowed to escape through the vent in the pot lid. (If necessary, add more water during the simmering process.) Drain. The muskrat meat may now be used in a recipe. For example, place the cut-up muskrat meat into a Dutch oven with 1 cup of water, 1 small chopped onion, 1/2 teaspoon salt, and 1/2 teaspoon thyme. Cover and simmer until the meat is tender and well done.

Opossum - (4 to 10 pounds, 3 feet long, long pointed nose, rat like tail) - Remove the internal organs of the opossum but do **not** skin it. Place the unskinned opossum in a pot of water and place the pot over the heat. Do **not** allow the water to boil. Periodically pull on the opossum's hair and when the hair comes out easily then remove the opossum from the water. Scrape the opossum and pour cool water over the opossum as you scrape. Remove the small red glands located in the small of the back and under each foreleg, between the shoulder and the ribs. Place the opossum meat in a large pot of cold water and bring slowly to a boil. Do **not** cover the pot. Allow it to simmer for 20 minutes. Drain. Place the opossum meat in a fresh pot of cold water and bring slowly to a boil. Do **not** cover the pot. Allow it to simmer for another 20 minutes. Drain off the hot water and then put the meat into some cold water to make it firm. The opossum meat may now be used in most recipes instead of pork or chicken.

Porcupine - (15 pounds, 3 feet long) - Hang the gutted porcupine in a cool dry area for two days. Then place it in a pot of salted water and allow the porcupine meat to soak for 12 hours inside the refrigerator. Remove the pot from the refrigerator. Place the pot over medium heat and bring to a boil. Drain and then put the meat into another pot of cold water and bring it to a boil. Drain. The porcupine meat may now be used in a recipe. For example, place the cut-up porcupine meat in a Dutch oven with 3 cups of water, 1/2 teaspoon pepper, 1 teaspoon salt, and some chopped onions and/or celery. Simmer for 2.5 hours.

Rabbit - (2 to 3 pounds) - Place the skinned cleaned rabbit in a pot of salted water for 12 hours inside the refrigerator. Rabbit may be used in place of chicken in almost any recipe. For example, cut-up rabbit pieces may be coated with salt, pepper, and flour, and then fried in a skillet like chicken.

Raccoon, also called a Coon - (15 pounds, 2 to 3 feet long, black mask around the eyes) - After removing all the fat on the outside and inside of the raccoon, place it in a pot of salted water and allow the meat to soak for 12 hours inside the refrigerator. Remove the pot from the refrigerator. Place the pot over medium heat and slowly bring the water to a boil. Then allow it to simmer for 45 minutes, without covering the pot. Add two tablespoons of baking soda to the water and continue to simmer for another five minutes. Drain off the hot water and then put the raccoon meat in a fresh pot of cold water and slowly bring to a boil. Allow it to simmer for 15 minutes. Drain off the hot water and then put the meat into some cold water to make it firm. The raccoon meat may now be used in most recipes instead of pork.

Squirrel - (Gray squirrels taste better than red squirrels.) Skin the squirrel remove and discard the digestive organs (stomach and intestines), and cut the squirrel into sections (legs, etc.). Cut the heart and liver into bite size pieces.

Squirrel Stew
Simmer all the meat in some hot water with a teaspoon of salt. When tender, remove the meat from the bones, dice it, and cook it a little longer. Add salt, pepper, onions, potatoes, and/or other vegetables, if available. Enjoy the meaty soup and drink the soup broth when the meat is gone.

Fried Squirrel
Soak the cut up squirrel meat in some water with one teaspoon of salt overnight. Then put it in a skillet with some salted water and slowly boil the meat until it is tender when stuck with a fork. Be very careful and do **not** cook the meat until it falls off the bones. Rinse the squirrel in some cold water.

| 1/2 cup flour | 1/2 tsp. salt | 1/2 tsp. pepper | 1/4 cup oil |

Mix the flour, salt, and pepper inside a zipper plastic baggie. Dip the pieces of squirrel meat in some milk (or water) and shake the meat inside the baggie to coat the meat. Brown the coated meat in some oil in a skillet. Lower the heat after browning and cover the skillet tightly. Cook over low heat for 30 to 60 minutes or until well done. Remove the cover during the last 10 minutes to crisp the outer surfaces.

Processing Instructions for Large Game Animals

Bear Meat - An adult black bear will weigh around 400 or 500 pounds. Bear should be hunted in the fall after it has had a chance to feed for an entire spring and summer. Do not hunt bear in the spring when it just becoming active after its winter hibernation because it will have lost a lot of weight and it may be somewhat parasitic.

Bear meat is relatively greasy and it may be used in place of pork or beef in recipes. After eating a properly prepared bear steak, some people have discovered they prefer the flavor of bear meat to beef.

Bear Fat - Properly rendered bear fat may be used in recipes in place of butter. Bear fat is richer than butter and therefore you should use a little less of it than the amount of butter specified in the recipe.

Remove the fat from the bear as soon as possible after the death of the bear. The fat will become rancid **very** quickly if it is not processed immediately. Cut the fat into small pieces and heat it slowly in a heavy large pot or pan that contains a small quantity of fresh water. If necessary, press down on the fat with a spoon to help it melt faster. After the fat has melted remove it from the heat and allow it to cool just a little. While it is still warm pour it through a cheesecloth and then store the melted fat in the refrigerator in a plastic storage container with a tight fitting lid.

The brown residue in the top of the cheesecloth is called "cracklings" and it may be saved and used as a flavoring in recipes.

Black Bear Roast - Slice bear meat into boneless one-pound steaks or into boneless roasts weighing between three to five pounds each. Allow the meat to soak overnight in the refrigerator in a marinade of four parts salted water to one part olive oil (or salad oil). Place the roast on a cooking rack that is one or two inches above the inside bottom of the roasting pan. Pour the marinade into the roasting pan on top of the roast. Add your favorite vegetables, such as sliced carrots, quartered potatoes, diced celery, or sliced onion. Add salt and pepper as desired. Bake in a 350°F oven for 90 minutes and then turn the roast over. Return to oven and bake an additional 90 minutes. Test to see if the meat is well done. In necessary, continue to cook for another 30 to 60 minutes. Remove roast and roasting rack from bottom of roasting pan. Set any vegetables aside. Pour remaining broth from roasting pan into a cook pot and bring to a boil on top of the stove. Add about 1/2 cup flour and stir to make gravy. Slice the roast and cover with gravy and then serve with vegetables.

Deer Meat (Venison) - Deer meat is very lean meat and it may be cooked, roasted, or broiled in the same manner as beef. It may be substituted for beef in almost any recipe. However, since it is a very lean meat it may require the addition of some fat or oil to the recipe.

Additional Cooking Suggestions

Broiling Meats over a Campfire
Sear the flesh of the animal over open flames before cooking. This keeps the juices and nutrients inside the animal.

Grilling Meats
Meats retain their juices better if they are turned 4 or 5 times while cooking. Turn meat with tongs not forks. Cook on grilling rack about 4 to 6 inches directly above the hot coals. The meat will cook quickly. Watch it closely.

Pan Steaks
Melt some fat in the frying pan. Salt and flour the steaks and put them in the pan. When the meat is almost ready, make some pan gravy by stirring a little flour in with the hot grease. Add a little water and stir to make pan gravy.

Wild Game Stew

Gut and skin the animal (deer, bear, beaver, raccoon, rabbit, porcupine, opossum) (or dog, cat, or something even less desirable in an emergency survival situation). Parboil the meat for about 10 minutes, allow it to cool, and then remove the meat from the bones. If present, cut off some fat and put it in the pot. While the fat is melting, cube the heart into small pieces and add it first. Skin the tongue and cube it and add it to the pot. This gives the 2 toughest pieces a longer time to cook. Cut up the liver and tenderloin and add them to the pot. Now cover everything with warm water and let it simmer. Add salt, pepper, and onion. Cooking time is three hours. The final stew is delicious.

Advantages of a Meat Grinder

Following are some reasons why you might wish to consider investing in a **stainless steel** meat grinder. A hand turned meat grinder has the following advantages:

1. Converts tough cuts of meat and wild game meat into hamburger consistency.
2. All red ground meat looks approximately the same.
3. Ground meat will minimize the number of future complaints you will hear from your family.
4. Ground meat is easier to use in a wider variety of recipes.
5. Ground meat more easily and completely absorbs any seasonings you may have.
6. Ground meat cooks faster and more thoroughly than thicker cuts of meat.
7. Ground meat is easier for most people to chew and it is easier for most people to digest.

You will also need some meat seasoning tenderizer, some chili seasoning, some taco seasoning, some Sloppy Joe seasoning, and any other seasonings that your family normally enjoys.

A Few Tips on How to Grind Meat

1. Chill the meat before grinding. Cold meat is easier to grind than meat at room temperature.
2. Cut the meat into cubes between one-half inch up to one-inch in size.
    a. If the meat does not contain much fat and you are adding fat from another source then cut the meat into one-half inch cubes.
    b. If you are blending two or more different types of meat together then cut the meat into one-half inch cubes.
3. Tender meat should be coarse ground.
4. A coarse grind is preferred for hamburgers because it helps the meat hold together while cooking.
5. Tough meat or meat with lots of sinews should be fine ground.
6. A fine grind helps the meat absorb the meat seasonings and to blend more evenly with other recipe ingredients.
7. If the meat is still too tough after grinding then put the ground meat through the meat grinder a second time.

Bone Marrow

The center of a bone contains marrow and it is edible. It is present in reasonable quantities in the spine and in the other large bones of game animals. The larger bones can be split and the marrow removed. Larger pieces of bone marrow may cut into 1/2 inch thick slices and then poached for 2 minutes, or it may be heated briefly in the top part of a double boiler.

Soup bones are frequently added to soup recipes to add nutrients and flavor. The bones are removed before serving the soup.

Chapter Thirty

How to Smoke Meat and How to Create Meat Jerky

There are some major differences in the methods that are used to smoke meat for immediate consumption and to smoke meat to extend is useful shelf life. If you are aware of these differences then you will be less likely to make the mistake of trying to smoke all meat the same way.

The variables of smoke, moisture, and heat need to be controlled differently for each of the following two applications:

1. **Smoking Meat so You can Eat it Now:** Requires some smoke, some moisture, and good heat.
2. **Smoking Meat for Long-Term Storage:** Requires some smoke, no moisture, and less heat.

In this chapter we will be describing how to smoke meat for long-term storage so we will be trying to produce a reasonable amount of smoke, but no moisture, and just the right amount of heat.

Instructions for Smoking Meat for Long-Term Storage

1. Slice the meat into strips in the same direction as the muscle. Each strip should be about one inch wide and 1/4 inch thick. The length isn't important. Trim off all the fat because the fat won't cure properly and it will spoil the meat.

2. **Optional** "brine" solution of salt and water -- If you intend to use the meat to make pemmican then you should **not** saturate the meat with salt until after you have added the other ingredients to the mixture. However, if your only objective is to simply preserve the meat as meat jerky then a salt brine soak is a very good idea because the salt and water solution will saturate into the meat and help to protect it. Soak the meat strips in one quart of water that contains 1/8 cup pure salt (not iodized salt). Soak the sliced meat in the salt solution for 30 to 60 minutes, depending on the thickness of the meat strips. Stir the meat strips inside the salt solution every 15 minutes to distribute the salt mixture onto all the surfaces of the meat. Several pounds of fresh thin meat strips can be processed in the salt and water solution at the same time. After removing the meat from the salt bath you may add your favorite seasoning to the meat, if you wish. However, seasoning is not needed if you smoke the meat because the smoke will overpower the seasoning.

3. **Optional** "string of meat" -- If you wish to create a string of meat, then push a clean thin wire, or a needle and some strong nylon thread, or a needle and some strong fishing line, through one end of each piece of meat. Each piece of meat should not touch itself or another piece of meat on the string of meat.

4. Dry the raw meat using any one of the following four methods.
   a. **Sun Drying Method:** Dry the raw meat using the heat of the sun, but not in direct sunlight. Support the meat by hanging it over a clean straight pole. Or hang a string of meat between two poles. Protect the meat strips with cheesecloth or screen wire so the birds can't eat them and the flies can't lay eggs on them. This is the method that was used by some Native American Indians. This method takes the most time and it does not put a protective smoke coating on the meat and it does not add the aroma and taste of the smoke to the meat.
   b. **Fire Pit and Smoke Method:** Dig a hole in the ground and start a fire in the hole. Or use some cement blocks or bricks to create a temporary small fire area that is protected from the wind. Put a metal grill on the blocks to support the meat. If you don't have a grill surface then support the meat by hanging it over a clean straight pole. Or hang a string of meat between two poles driven in the ground. Don't burn soft wood such as pine because the pine pitch will taint the meat. When the fire has burned down to hot coals then place the meat above the hot coals. The air should feel hot to your hand but it should not burn your hand. Do not cook the meat -- only dry the meat. Add some decayed wood or sawdust to the coals to make smoke. The smoke will put a protective coating on the meat. The heat and the smoke will keep the birds and flies away.

    c. **Smokehouse Method:** Hang a string of meat inside the smokehouse. Start a fire inside the Dutch oven in the smokehouse. Add some decayed wood or sawdust to the coals to make smoke. Maintain the temperature inside the smokehouse between 170° to 185° F (77° to 85° C) for 6 to 10 hours. The smoke will put a protective coating on the meat. The heat will destroy any harmful microorganisms in the meat. Do not cook the meat. You only want to dry the meat.

    d. **Oven Method:** Spread out the meat strips on aluminum foil on a cookie sheet and dry the meat inside an oven at a temperature between 170° to 185° F (77° to 85° C) for 6 to 10 hours. The heat will destroy any harmful microorganisms in the meat. Do not cook the meat -- only dry the meat. Turn the meat strips over every two hours so they dry evenly on both sides. This method does not put a protective smoke coating on the meat and it does not add the aroma and the taste of the smoke to the meat.

5. Periodically bend the meat jerky strips to test for dryness. Properly dried meat jerky will crack or snap when bent. If it bends without cracking then it still contains too much moisture. If it crumbles then it is too dry. It will still be edible but it will have lost some of its nutritional value.

6. Store the dried meat jerky in a container to protect it from insects. Properly dried meat jerky is safe to eat for up to one year. It may be eaten dry but **it tastes better if it is dipped in water for a short time just before eating.** Or use the meat jerky in a stew.

How Much Time is Required to Dry The Meat?

It is not possible to predict the amount of time required to dry the meat because there are four different methods that can be used, and there are too many different variables that impact the actual time that will be needed.

For example,
1. The thickness of the meat strips.
2. The amount of moisture in the meat strips.
3. The size of the original fire, if drying above a fire.
4. The type of wood used to build the original fire, if drying above a fire.
5. The distance the meat strips are placed above the coals of the fire, if drying by a fire or in a smokehouse.
6. The amount of heat generated by the red hot coals in the fire pit or in the smokehouse.
7. The air temperature 10 feet away from the fire or outside the smokehouse (30° F, 70° F, 105° F, etc.).
8. The normal humidity in the air about ten feet away from the fire, if drying above a fire.

Therefore to determine if the meat is done you must bend each strip of meat. If it cracks or snaps it is done. If it bends easily it is not done.

1. The meat directly above the very center of the fire will usually dry faster than the meat near the outside edges of the fire.
2. The meat near the outside edges of the fire will usually take a little longer to dry properly.
3. The **thinner** meat strips will usually dry a little faster.
4. The **thicker** meat strips will usually take a little longer to dry properly.

You will probably discover that you will not be removing all the meat strips from above the fire, or from the smokehouse, or from the oven, at the same time. Instead you will be selectively removing specific meat strips as they become dry enough and you will be leaving some of the other meat strips above the fire, or in the smokehouse, or in the oven, for a slightly longer period of time.

Chapter Thirty-One

Grandpappy's Pemmican Recipe
A Native American Indian Survival Food

Pemmican is a Native American Indian survival food that has a very long shelf life and it requires no refrigeration. It is similar to a Granola Bar except it contains no artificial preservatives. It is a compact energy source that contains protein, fiber, fat, carbohydrates, natural fruit sugars, vitamins, and minerals. It also tastes great because it is a simple combination of meat jerky and your favorite dried fruit.

To make pemmican you only need three basic ingredients:

1. lean meat,
2. animal fat, and
3. fruit or berries.

Pemmican has several very important and desirable characteristics:

1. It uses both the lean meat and the fat from an animal.
2. It conveniently stores your summer food harvest for winter consumption.
3. It requires no refrigeration or canning jars for safe long-term food storage.
4. It does not weigh very much because it contains no significant moisture.
5. It is a complete meal all by itself.
6. It is very nutritious and very tasty.
7. It can easily be made in the wilderness without any special cookware or equipment.

The following recipe uses equal amounts of dried lean meat, dried fruit, and melted fat. However, pemmican is a very flexible food and you can vary the quantities of these three basic ingredients to more fully utilize almost all of whatever food you may have available. For example:

1. Most animals have a lot of lean meat but very little fat. In this situation you should only use just enough melted fat to hold your pemmican together.
2. Depending on the weather conditions the summer wild fruit and berry harvest may be excellent or very poor. Depending on what you actually have available each summer you could use more or less dried fruit or berries in the recipe.
3. During the summer when wild game and berries are widely available you can harvest as much as you can and then process it all into pemmican for winter consumption when little or no food will be available. This is the reason pemmican was such an important survival food for the Native American Indians.
4. If you have more lean meat than you can use then you can simply convert the extra lean meat into meat jerky.
5. If you have more dried fruit than you can use then you can simply save the extra dried fruit for winter consumption.
6. If you have very little animal fat then it is possible to make a simple granola snack for winter consumption by mixing some dried meat and dried fruit together without using any melted animal fat. However, if you have animal fat then you should use it because animal fat is a necessary food for long-term survival.

Instructions for Making Pemmican

Basic Ingredients:
1 Cup of Dried Meat
1 Cup of Dried Fruit or Berries
1 Cup of Melted Animal Fat

Meat: Use deer, moose, caribou, or beef, but not pork. It takes between one to two pounds of fresh meat to make one cup of dried meat. The meat should be as lean as possible. Trim off **all** the fat. Cut the fresh meat into wafer thin slices about 1/4 inch thick or a little thinner.

Do **not** add salt at this time. Do **not** soak the meat in a solution of salt and water. This is **not** the best time to add salt if you are making pemmican. Salt should be added later in this recipe.

Use either one of the following two methods to process the fresh meat:

1. If you have a meat grinder then grind the fresh meat twice. Spread the ground meat evenly on aluminum foil on a cookie sheet and dry inside an oven at 185 degrees Fahrenheit (85 degrees Centigrade) for 3 to 5 hours, or until it is crisp and chewy. Stir the meat every hour. Don't cook the meat -- just dry it.

2. If you don't have a meat grinder then spread the meat strips evenly and separately on aluminum foil on a cookie sheet and dry the sliced meat inside an oven at 185 degrees Fahrenheit (85 degrees Centigrade) for 6 to 10 hours, or until it is crisp and chewy. Turn the meat strips over every two hours so they will dry evenly on both sides. You do not want to cook the meat. You only want to dry it. If the meat snaps or cracks when bent it is done. If it bends it still contains too much moisture. If it crumbles it is too dry but it can still be used.

Grind or crush the dried meat almost into a powder. If you have an electric blender then blend the meat into a fine pulp.

Fruit or Berries: Use one or two types of fruit or berries, such as blueberries, huckleberries, currants, raisins, apples, apricots, or cherries. Cut the fruit into thin slices or pieces and dry them using the heat of the sun. Or dry them in the oven at the same time you dry your meat jerky. Or use an electric food dehydrator. Grind the dried fruit into a powder but leave some of it a little lumpy to provide for extra texture and taste.

Mix the dried meat powder and the dried fruit powder together in a bowl. If you have an electric blender then add the dried fruit to the dried meat in the blender and mix them together.

Optional Salt: If you have salt then you should stir some salt into the mixture to enhance its flavor. The addition of salt at this time will distribute the salt throughout the mixture which includes both the dried meat powder and the dried fruit powder so the salt can help to protect both ingredients. Salt will increase the shelf life of the pemmican and it will help to retard the future growth of harmful microorganisms that may try to attack the pemmican from the surrounding environment. The salt will **not** kill those microorganisms but it will help to keep them from multiplying. If you do not have any salt then you should keep your pemmican in a sealed glass jar, or a sealed food grade plastic storage container, or a sealed heavy-duty plastic zipper freezer bag in order to help protect it from any harmful microorganisms that may be present in the surrounding air.

Optional Ingredients: Add a little honey. Or add some minced dried onion for flavor. Or add a few crushed nuts. However, nuts contain oil and the nuts will shorten the shelf life of your pemmican. When adding these optional ingredients you should begin with a very small batch of pemmican. This will permit you to experiment and determine if the results are agreeable to your family's taste requirements without ruining a huge batch of pemmican.

Optional Granola Snack: If you have nuts, such as acorns, then a better use for them would be to crush them and mix them with your extra left-over dried meat and dried fruit to make a granola type stack. Granola is *easy* to mix together if you have the ingredients and therefore it should **not** be prepared before you are ready to eat it. If you prepare it too soon and one of your ingredients goes bad then it will ruin all your granola. But if you wait until you are ready to eat it then you can easily detect the bad ingredient and discard it and not put it into your granola mix.

Animal Fat: Use fresh beef fat or pork fat or any hard fat. Animal fat will quickly become rancid and it should be melted (rendered) as soon as possible. Cut the fat into 1/8 inch to 1/4 inch cubes and melt it over medium-low heat in a very small amount of clean rainwater in a clean cook pot. Do not allow it to smoke. If it starts to smoke then you are burning the fat.

When the fat is completely melted gradually pour it over the meat-fruit mixture in the bowl and stir until the mixture is well coated and sticks together. Then spread it out like dough and allow it to cool completely. When cool cut it into pieces about 1 inch wide and 4 inches long.

If possible, wrap the pemmican in plastic wrap or store it in Ziploc bags or in plastic storage containers with a tight fitting lid. Pemmican can be safely stored for 8 months. If you can keep the temperature between 40°F to 75°F (or 4°C to 24°C) then pemmican can be stored for a longer period of time.

Salt Footnote: Salt does **not** kill or neutralize the harmful microorganisms that may be present in the meat or the fruit. Salt only inhibits their future growth. Any harmful microorganisms that might be present will be killed by the heat during the meat drying process, and during the fruit drying process, and during the fat melting process.

Optional "Brine" Solution of Salt and Water for Meat Jerky: If you have more lean meat than dried fruit then you could convert the extra lean meat into meat jerky. After slicing the meat into thin strips you could soak the meat strips in one-quart of water that contains 1/8 cup salt. Soak the sliced meat in the salt solution for 30 to 60 minutes, depending on the thickness of the meat strips. Stir the meat strips inside the salt solution every 15 minutes to achieve a good distribution of the salt mixture onto all the surfaces of the meat. Several pounds of fresh thin meat strips can be processed in the salt water solution at the same time. If your only objective is to preserve the meat then a salt brine soak is a very good idea because the salt water solution will saturate into the meat and help to protect it.

Salt and Pemmican: However, if you are making pemmican then you should **not** soak the meat in a salt brine solution. If you saturate the meat with salt then the meat will have a very salty taste and you will **not** be able to add more salt later. The reason salt should be added later is because it is better to equally distribute the salt throughout the entire pemmican mixture, including the dried meat, the dried fruit, and the melted animal fat. Therefore if you are making pemmican then you should dry the meat and grind it into tiny pieces or a powder. Then dry the fruit and grind it into tiny pieces or a powder. Mix the meat and fruit together and then add some salt. The salt will be able to make contact with all the surfaces of the meat, and with the fruit, and later with the hot melted animal fat. This is the **best** way to add salt when making pemmican because the salt will help to protect the entire pemmican wafer bar instead of just protecting the meat inside the bar.

Technical Footnote: Neither sodium nitrite, nor sodium chloride (table salt), nor a brine solution will neutralize all the harmful microorganisms that could be present in fresh meat. In fact, the scientific experiment summarized at *http://lib.bioinfo.pl/pmid:952* reported that **sodium nitrate only slowed down the growth** of *Salmonella* and *Staphylococcus* on hot dogs and the sodium nitrite did **not** slow the growth rate of these harmful microorganisms by a significant amount.

On the other hand, it has been repeatedly documented that **heat** will destroy almost every harmful microorganism that might be present in meat. For example, in beef, venison, and other red meats:

1. *Salmonella* is destroyed at a temperature of 165 degrees Fahrenheit (74° Centigrade).

2. *Listeria monocytogenes* is destroyed at a temperature of 160 degrees Fahrenheit (71° Centigrade).

3. *Staphylococcus aureus* is destroyed at a temperature of 140 degrees Fahrenheit (60° Centigrade).

4. *Escherichia coli* is destroyed at a temperature of 165 degrees Fahrenheit (74° Centigrade).

Chapter Thirty-Two

Hot and Cold Beverages

Baby Formula (8 ounce bottle)

6 tbsp. nonfat dry milk	2 tsp. olive or vegetable oil
1 cup water (safe or boiled)	1 tsp. sugar

Mix will. Serve at room temperature or slightly warmed. Test a small drop on your wrist before feeding to the baby.
If there are no baby bottles available then feed the baby using a spoon or a sterile eye-dropper or a sterile medicine-dropper.
Caution: Do **not** use corn syrup or honey instead of the sugar. They both contain potential bacteria which can kill a young baby who does not have a fully developed immune system.

Electrolyte Beverage (Gatorade, Pedialyte)

1 quart water	1/2 tsp. baking soda
1 tsp. Lite salt	6 to 10 tsp. granulated sugar

Optional Ingredient: Package of Kool-Aid for color and flavoring.
Mix well. Replaces lost electrolytes due to dehydration (diarrhea, vomiting, excessive sweating, etc.).

Hot Chocolate or Chocolate Milk

1 tbsp. cocoa powder	2 tbsp. sugar	pinch of salt
1/3 cup instant nonfat dry milk	1 cup water, either hot or cold	

Combine everything in water, either hot or cold, and stir well.

Chocolate Milkshake

4 tsp. chocolate syrup	2 tbsp. sugar
1/3 cup instant nonfat dry milk	1 cup cold water

Combine everything and chill.

Peanut Butter Milkshake

3 tbsp. peanut butter	2 tbsp. sugar
1/3 cup instant nonfat dry milk	1 cup cold water

Blend everything using a food blender. Chill and serve.

Chilled Rice Beverage or Milkshake

2 cups **cooked** white rice	2 tbsp. honey
2 cups low fat milk	1/4 tsp. ground cinnamon

Combine all ingredients in a jar and shake vigorously. Refrigerate for 4 hours or overnight.
For a rice **beverage**, strain the rice to separate out the liquid. Fill two glasses with ice and pour the

liquid over the ice. Serve chilled. (Note: You may use the rice in a potluck pie.)
For a rice **milkshake**, do not strain but pour the rice and liquid mixture into a blender and blend until creamy. Serve cold.

Russian Tea

1 cup instant tea	2 cups Tang	3 cups sugar	1 tsp. cinnamon

Preparation: Mix all the above dry ingredients and store in an air-tight plastic container.
Cook: Add 2 tsp. of the above mixture to one cup of hot water and stir.

Clover Tea

Dried clover leaves and blossoms

Preparation: Collect clover leaves and blossoms when mature. Dry at room temperature. When thoroughly dry, crush or rub into very small particles. Store in an airtight jar or plastic container.
Cook: Add 1 tsp. to one cup of boiling water and stir.
Option: May be sweetened with honey.

Chapter Thirty-Three

Introduction to Homemade Alcoholic Beverages

Always obey your local, state, and national laws and regulations that pertain to alcohol production and consumption. These rules and laws do change occasionally so you will need to determine what the current laws are and then you should obey those laws.

At the beginning of the year 2011 in the United States of America an adult could legally make a limited amount of both of the following alcoholic beverages for consumption by his or her own family (and which are not offered for sale to anyone):

1. Wine: Fermentation of grapes or fruits.
2. Beer: Fermentation of barley.

If you currently enjoy a specific brand name alcoholic beverage then the chance of your being able to perfectly replicate that taste yourself is extremely small. On the other hand, if you are reasonably flexible in your tastes then you could make any one of the above two beverages at home.

Wine: In my opinion wine is the easiest of the two beverages to make at home. You only need the grapes or the fruit, a fermentation bottle (such as a one-gallon wine bottle), a 12-inch diameter balloon (the type used at children's parties), and a little extra white granulated sugar (or the sugar water from sugar beets). If you have a good wine recipe, such as the one that appears in this book, then you can make good quality homemade wine that has a very agreeable taste.

Beer: Although it is possible to make beer at home, you will need to invest in a variety of beer making items and some beer yeast and hops. It is possible to grow your own barley and then convert it into malt, or you could buy the malted barley. You can also grow your own hops. Homemade beer making kits are also available that come in cans and you just add water and yeast and follow the directions.

Over a three-year period I tried a wide variety of beer recipes from several different books and from several different local homebrew shops where their clientele shared their favorite beer making recipes. Although I always followed the directions without any personal modifications, I was never happy with any of the beer I brewed at home. Then I started modifying the recipes and I tried to develop a beer that would taste approximately like an American made smooth light beer. Although I eventually ended up with my own recipe for an average tasting beer, I was never able to even get close to the taste of an American made light beer. Therefore I don't make beer anymore. The reason I am sharing my personal failure in this area is so you don't criticize yourself too harshly if you decide to try your luck at homebrewing and you also eventually discover that you don't like your own beer as much as a name brand beer. However, in order to be of some assistance to you if you decide to begin this adventure, I have included my beer making recipe in this book. My beer making recipe is the result of three years of experimentation from 1995 to 1997 in the homebrewing process and it would be a reasonable starting position for someone who desires to create a mild smooth tasting light beer.

(Note: Between the years of 2002 to 2008 I worked as an occasional part-time quality training consultant for Anheuser Busch in their Georgia, New York, and Virginia breweries. During this seven-year period I had the opportunity to meet and talk with a wide variety of brewing professionals who had spent a good part of their adult lives working for Anheuser Busch. A professional brewery has equipment and procedures that very accurately and precisely control every step in the brewing process. There is simply no way an individual could hope to come even close to the precision brewing methods used by a commercial brewery. I mention this so that you will hopefully set realistic expectations for your homebrewed beer and not make the same mistake I made of trying to closely match the taste of a beer made by a huge brewery.)

Spirits: There are a variety of laws and regulations about the production of high percentage alcohol and you should review those laws and regulations and comply with all of them. High percentage alcohol will require an investment in an alcohol still and some good yeast that is specifically designed for the type of alcohol you wish to make. One internet web site that sells alcohol stills and alcohol yeast is the following:

http://www.milehidistilling.com   Telephone Number: (303) 987-3955

Two very good books on how to distill grains into alcohol are the following:

1. **Making Pure Corn Whiskey**, Ian Smiley BSc, 2003
2. **The Compleat Distiller**, Second Edition, Nixon and McCaw, 2004

Although it was mentioned above, please let me remind you that even if you have all the necessary equipment to make wine, beer, or spirits, but you do **not** have any raw materials (grapes, barley, grains), then you will **not** be able to make alcohol.

Chapter Thirty-Four

Grandpappy's Homemade Beer Recipes

Five Gallons of Light Beer	**Three Gallons of Light Beer**
4 Pounds Pale Barley Malt	2.5 Pounds Pale Barley Malt
0.75 Pounds Crystal Malt	0.5 Pounds Crystal Malt
0.5 Pounds White Rice (Optional)	0.3 Pounds White Rice (Optional)
1.5 Ounces Cascade Hops (7.5 HBU)	1 Ounce Cascade Hops (5 HBU)
Beer Yeast	Beer Yeast
7 Gallons Pure Water	4.5 Gallons Pure Water
1/3 Teaspoon Irish Moss (Optional)	1/4 Teaspoon Irish Moss (Optional)

Note: HBU = (ounces of hops) x (alpha percent of hops)
Note: Hallertauer Hops or Mt. Hood Hops may be used instead of Cascade Hops.
Note: Pale and Crystal Malts may be purchased from a Brewing Supply Store. If you do not have access to Pale and Crystal Malts then you may substitute Barley seed in place of both of the above malts. The following recipe begins with barley seed instead of the two types of Barley Malts.

Malted Barley: (Note: Skip this step if you purchased barley malt and crystal malt.) Your barley seed must first be sprouted. Rinse the seeds thoroughly in clean water and then soak the seeds overnight in cool water using four times the amount of water as barley seeds. The next morning drain the seeds and place them on a shallow dish or pan and keep them moist (not wet). A thin layer of seeds is better than a deep layer of seeds. Sprinkle lightly with water twice a day. Seeds sprout quite well at a typical room temperature between 60°F to 90°F (15.5°C to 32°C). When the sprouts are the same length as the original seed then the sprouts should be heated in a 185°F to 230°F (85°C to 110°C) oven for a few minutes. Or the sprouts can be put inside a fine mesh laundry bag (or inside nylon pantyhose with the top of the pantyhose tied shut) and tumbled inside a clothes dryer for a few minutes. The malted barely is now ready to be converted into beer.

Grinding (Making the Grist): Put a small quantity of malted barley (called the malt) in the barley mill (a flour mill will be okay but **not** a coffee mill or a meat grinder). Grind the malt to break up the husk. Do **not** grind it into fine flour. One cup of crushed barley malt (called the grist) weighs about one-fourth pound. The grist should be used within 24-hours of grinding.

Optional Rice Adjunct (Note: Short grain white rice is better than long grain for brewing beer.): Course grind the white rice in a barley mill. Boil the ground white rice in 3 quarts of water for about 30 minutes to gelatinize it. Stir the rice every 1 or 2 minutes or it will burn and stick to the bottom of the pot. Turn off the heat. Let the rice syrup cool uncovered. After cooling for 30 minutes you may add up to 1 quart of very cold water to help the temperature drop to 140°F (60°C). (Note: Rice will lighten the taste and make the beer taste more like a typical American beer. Rice has a neutral flavor, the highest alcohol yield, and the lowest level of bad tasting proteins of any type of grain.) (Note: Do not exceed a 1 to 5 ratio of rice to barley, or 1 pound of rice per 5 pounds of barley, or you will have a sticky mash which will probably result in a stuck sparge runoff, or a minimum of a 3 to 5-hour sparge.)

Protease Rest: Gradually pour some of the barley grist into the rice syrup and stir. Continue adding grist and stirring until all the grist is in the pot. (If necessary, add hot water to obtain a wet oatmeal appearance. Avoid a dry oatmeal appearance.) Adjust the temperature of the mixture to between 125° to 130°F (52.5°C to 54.5°C). Turn off the heat. Put the lid on the kettle and let it stand for 30 minutes. After 30 minutes, add heat to bring the grist mixture to 154° to 156°F (68°C to 69°C).

Mashing or Striking: Turn off the heat. Put the lid on the pot. Check the temperature every 30 minutes (it should be 150°F (65.5°C) or above). Add heat when needed to increase the temperature (and stir while heating to prevent burning). Turn off the heat and replace the lid. The mash temperature should be held between 150°F and 158°F (65.5°C to 70°C) for 90 minutes. The ideal temperature is 152°F (67°C). This allows the conversion of starch into sugar to take place at the optimal rate. The pH should be between 5.2 to 5.5.

Optional Iodine Test for Starch Conversion: Put 1 teaspoon of mash liquid in a white saucer and cool it down. Add 1 drop of iodine. If the iodine does not change color then starch conversion is complete. If it turns black, dark blue, or purple then continue to mash at 152°F (67°C) for 10 more minutes and test again. Always discard the iodine test solution. Do **not** put the poisonous iodine test solution back into the mash. (Note: Starch left in the mash will cause chill haze in the finished beer.)

Mash Out: Add heat to increase the mash temperature to 165° to 168°F (74°C to 75.5°C). Put the lid on the pot and let the mash rest for 15 minutes. Then add heat to bring the mash temperature up to 170°F (76.5°C).

Lautering or Vorlauf: Put 1 quart of 170°F (76.5°C) water (from a separate pot) into the bottom of a five-gallon drinking water cooler that has a false bottom with holes. Transfer the mash from the mash pot to the cooler. Drain off 1 quart of mash liquid and sprinkle it over the mash. Repeat three more times until the mash liquid is relatively clear. Then stop recirculating the mash liquid. Instead transfer the mash liquid to the wort kettle where you will later boil your wort. Turn the heat on very low under the wort kettle.

Do **not** aerate the mash liquid when transferring it from the cooler to the wort kettle. Pour the liquid into the wort kettle from a height of less than one-inch. Collect enough mash/sparge liquid (called wort) for a good boil. Five quarts of liquid will boil down to 4 quarts (or one-gallon) of finished beer.

Boiling the Wort: Apply full heat to the wort kettle and **partially** cover the kettle. Wait for the wort to come to a boil. The boil the wort for 30 minutes. The boil should be a rolling boil, not just a slight simmering boil. A hard boil is absolutely necessary to avoid a multitude of potential problems. Then add 1 ounce of **bittering hops** to the wort (or 0.6 ounces for 3 gallons) and continue boiling for another 45 minutes in a partially covered kettle. Do **not** put the hops in a hop bag. Do **not** completely cover the kettle or it will boil over. Stir the wort every few minutes to keep it from sticking to the bottom of the kettle.

Add 0.25 ounces **of finishing (flavoring) hops** (or 0.2 ounces for 3 gallons), and add the Irish Moss if available, and boil the wort for an additional 10 minutes. The Irish Moss will help eliminate bad tasting undesirable proteins.

Add 0.25 ounces of aroma hops (or 0.2 ounces for 3 gallons), and boil for one-minute. Turn off the heat. Put the lid completely on the kettle. Let the covered wort steep for two-minutes.

Cooling: Remove the lid from the kettle and cool the wort as quickly as possible to between 60 to 75°F (15.5°C to 24°C). Do **not** aerate the wort while it is hot.

Aeration and Trub Removal: After the wort has cooled, and before the yeast is added, the wort must be aerated (oxygen added). This can be done in either of two ways as follows:

(a) If leaf hops were used then spoon some of the hops into a strainer and then slowly pour the wort through the hops in the strainer and into the primary fermenter. The loose hops will serve as a natural filter to catch some of the waste products from the boil (called **trub**.)
(b) Stir the wort to create a whirlpool in the center of the wort. The hops and the trub will collect in the center of the kettle. Wait about 15 minutes. Then siphon the wort from the edge of the kettle into the primary fermenter. Then shake the wort inside the fermenter to aerate it. Shake it a lot, or pour it from one container to another at least two times.

Chapter Thirty-Four: Beer

Priming Liquid: Before adding the yeast, remove some of the cooled wort for later use as priming liquid (instead of corn sugar). Remove approximately 1.67 quarts of cooled wort (called **gyle**) and set it aside in a covered jar in the refrigerator (or 1 quart for 3 gallons). Prior to capping you will need one-ounce (or two-tablespoons) of gyle to prime each 12 ounce bottle for carbonation. The formula is:

Quarts of Gyle = (12 x Gallons of Wort) / [(Initial SG − 1.000) x 1000]

Pitching the Yeast: Put the **beer yeast** in the cooled wort and stir. (See the yeast footnote at the end of this chapter.) Do **not** use bread yeast or wine yeast. Attach the fermentation lock and begin fermentation in the primary fermenter, which is usually a 6.5 gallon plastic bucket with a tight lid.

Foam Removal: After about 16 to 24 hours, skim the dirty foam (called **scum**) off the top of the beer. This dirty scum contains the cold break trub and if it falls back into the beer it may make a light beer taste more bitter. The yeast will also feed on it and that is very undesirable. Only skim the foam one time. The foam is the yeast at work. Lager yeast is top working yeast and it rises to the top of the beer. The second layer of foam that forms is the new, young yeast, and it is the best thing for achieving maximum beer flavor. (You can harvest half of the second layer of foam for recycling the yeast. See the continuous brewing footnote at the end of this chapter).

Dry Hopping (Optional): Put 1 additional ounce of fresh hops in a hop bag (or nylon stocking) and put it into the primary fermenter. The will add a distinctive hop aroma to your beer. (Be sure you can get the hop bag out of the fermenter when you are finished brewing. In other words, don't force the hop bag into the small mouth of a carboy bottle, if it used as a primary fermenter. Divide the hops into smaller bags that can be more easily removed when the time comes.) Don't transfer the hop bag to the secondary fermenter.

Racking: Siphon the beer into the secondary fermenter after 2 or 3 days. The secondary fermenter is usually a glass carboy with a fermentation lock. The ideal fermentation temperature is between 60°F to 74°F (15.5°C to 23.5°C). If the fermentation temperature is too high then put the fermenter in a tub of cool tap water. Wrap a towel around the fermenter so it hangs down into the water. The towel will absorb water and the water will evaporate and this will cool the fermenter about 2°F to 3°F (1°C) lower than the water in the tub. Ferment in a dark place (or wrap the fermenter with a towel).

Bottling: When fermentation has stopped in the secondary fermenter (another 4 to 10 days), prepare your bottles by putting two-tablespoons (one-ounce) of gyle in each sterilized 12-ounce beer bottle. Siphon the beer into the bottle within one-half inch of the top with beer and then cap the bottle. Age the bottled beer for at least six-weeks. The flavor of the beer will improve with age. (If you are going to store your beer for more than four months then you should double the hopping rate to improve its shelf life.)

Yeast Footnote

Dried Yeast (7 to 15 grams per 5 gallons of beer): Dried yeast should be rehydrated before adding it to the wort. Boil 12 ounces of water and let it cool to 95°F (35°C). Add the yeast and let it stand for 20 minutes. Then stir the rehydrated yeast into the wort. (Do **not** put dried yeast into the gyle. Dried yeast only needs water. Gyle will slow it down and impair it.)

Liquid Yeast: Follow the instructions on the package. Lay the package on the counter and hit it with your palm to break the inner seal. Knead the package to mix the contents. Shake the package. Let the package stand at room temperature (70° to 80°F or 21°C to 27°C) for one-day. After the package swells up pour the yeast into one-pint of gyle or malt extract and let it stand for 12 hours. Then pitch it into the wort.

Note: Yeast gives superior results if it is reused only once. The best way to do this is to salvage the yeast from the bottom of a home brewed beer bottle that was brewed from virgin yeast used straight

Chapter Thirty-Four: Beer

from the package. Slowly pour off most of the beer and then pour the remaining yeast slurry (the bottom one-half inch of beer in the bottle) into any sanitized glass container. Add one cup of gyle at room temperature (70° to 80°F or 21°C to 27°C) to the yeast slurry to bring it back to life. Don't rush the yeast. Wait for the top layer of foam to appear before adding another cup of gyle. It will take several hours (maybe days). After you have six cups of fermenting gyle, pour it into 3 or 5 gallons of fresh wort. Liquid yeast gives better results than dry yeast when it comes to recycling. Dry yeast gives relatively poor results when recycled but it is still superior to bread yeast.

Continuous Brewing Footnote

Brew your beer based on how you drink your beer. If you drink 3 gallons per week, then brew 3 gallons per week (or brew six-gallons every two weeks). If you drink 5 gallons per week, then brew 5 gallons per week. Start brewing your next batch of beer when you are ready to bottle your last batch of beer. This has two significant benefits as follows:

1. You can recycle your yeast. You must first remove and discard the first dirty layer of foam (scum) from the top of your last batch of fermenting beer. Then remove about half of the second layer of foam that forms on top of the beer and save it in any sterile glass container by putting some previously fully fermented beer on top of it (about 1 inch of beer) and then put it in the refrigerator at about 33° to 35°F (0.5°C to 1.5°C). When you need the yeast, gently pour off most of the beer and mix the remaining yeast slurry into 1.5 quarts of gyle at room temperature and wait 12 to 24 hours. Then mix the reactivated yeast solution with a new batch of cooled wort to start fermentation. (If possible, yeast should be used with 7 days of when it was first collected for best results).

2. You can also use some of the cooled wort from your next batch of beer (before adding the yeast) as the gyle to prime the bottles from your last batch of beer. This eliminates the need to store priming gyle in your refrigerator. (However, you will need a supply of gyle for recycling your yeast, so keep some gyle in your refrigerator for that purpose.)

This is not difficult. Think it through and you will see that it is a superior way to brew beer for year round consumption. The only problem you may encounter is during the summer months if refrigeration is not available. Then you would have to brew more in the cool months of the fall, winter, and spring for consumption during the hot months of summer. But you need to plan ahead in this scenario and put aside several good bottles of highly hopped beer with good yeast in it (stored in a very cool place) for recycling the yeast the following fall. If you don't then you will lose your yeast.

Chapter Thirty-Five

Grandpappy's Homemade Wine Recipes

Introduction

During hard times it is possible to make beer and wine at home. Of these two alcoholic beverages, wine is the preferred hard times beverage for the following reasons:

1. Wine is much easier to make than beer.
2. Wine making requires very little equipment -- just a fermentation bottle and either a 9-inch or a 12-inch diameter balloon.
3. The fermentation temperature does not need to be precisely controlled.
4. Wine (12%) has an average alcohol content that is higher than beer (6%) but lower than liquor (40%).
5. Wine can be made from a variety of different fruits, grapes, and berries, including wild blackberries, raspberries, and huckleberries (wild blueberries).
6. Wine can be made from the flower blossoms of some weeds that grow wild and abundantly in nature, such as dandelions and kudzu.
7. Wine can be made from sweet sugar beet water.
8. Wine can be made using ordinary bread yeast or wild yeast that is already present on the fruit.
9. During hard times it is a good idea to remember that "*wine makes glad the heart of man.*" (Psalm 104:15) A little wine may help to take your mind of the depressing situations that exist all around you.

For all the above reasons wine is the alcoholic beverage of choice during a hard times tragedy event.

Grandpappy's Basic Wine Recipe for One Gallon of Wine

3 Pounds of Fully Ripe Fruit (the fruit really needs to be fully and completely ripe).
1 Package of Wine or Champagne Yeast (or Bread Yeast or Wild Yeast).
3 Quarts Spring Water or Well Water (contains necessary minerals and nutrients).
3/4 Teaspoon Yeast Nutrient or Yeast Energizer (Step 13) (Optional).
2 Campden Tablets (Steps 11 and 19) (Optional).
4 Cups Sugar (Granulated, Powder, or Brown) (Step 8) (Optional but highly desirable).
1 Cup Sugar (1/2 Cup at Step 22 and 1/2 Cup at Step 26) (Optional but highly desirable).
5 Raisins (Step 23) (Optional).

Water: Do **not** use chlorinated tap water. Do **not** use distilled water because it contains no minerals.

Fruits and Berries: Approximately three-pounds of apricots, bananas, peaches, plums, blackberries, blueberries, cranberries, elderberries, gooseberries, huckleberries, raspberries, or strawberries will make one-gallon of good wine.

Pears: It takes about four-pounds of pears to make one-gallon of wine.

Grapes: It takes about six-pounds of bunch grapes or muscadine grapes to make one-gallon of good wine. Therefore during hard times grapes could be converted into either wine or jelly.

Apples and Cherries: It takes about 15 pounds of apples or about 6 pounds of cherries to make one gallon of wine. Therefore apples and cherries should probably be used in some other way during really hard times.

Sugar Beet Wine: If you have "sweet sugar beet water" then mix two-quarts of the sweet sugar beet water with two-quarts of well water or spring water and start at Step Number 12 below.

Sugar Substitute: Sweet sugar beet water may be used in Steps 8, 22, and 26 instead of refined cane sugar.

Sugar Weight and Volume: One-pound of cane sugar is approximately two-cups of cane sugar.

Grandpappy's Winemaking Note: I always use well water and sugar and raisins. And I frequently use wild yeast instead of package yeast. But I normally do **not** use yeast nutrient, or campden tablets, or a hydrometer.

The Basic Wine Making Steps

1. **Fully Ripe Fruit:** Rinse the fully ripe fruit, berries, or grapes to remove any foreign particles, dirt, or dust.

2. **Freezing:** Freeze the fruit for 24 hours. Then thaw the fruit. (Note: Freezing increases the juice extraction yield percentage from fresh fruit.)

3. **Seed Removal:** Remove the seeds, pit, or core from the fruit (apples, cherries, grapes, peaches, pears, or plums). The seeds will transmit an unpleasant taste to the wine if you do not remove them at this time. (Note: It took three hours to cut six pounds of muscadine grapes into quarters and remove all the seeds.)

4. **Juice Extraction:** Process the fruit and extract its juice. Smash, crush, or squeeze the fruit or grapes or berries to extract as much juice as possible. Do **not** process the fruit in a blender or juicer because this will add too much bitterness from the skins and fruit pulp into the juice.

5. **Soaking:** Allow the skins and pulp to mix with the juice inside a large clean sterile bucket or stock pot for either two days or for six days. If you intend to use a package yeast then limit the soaking time to two days to prevent the wild yeast from multiplying significantly inside the juice. If you intend to use a wild yeast then wait the full six days to give the wild yeast a chance to firmly establish itself in the juice. Cover the bucket with a towel to keep the contents clean and to keep insects and flies out. The longer the pulp soaks inside the juice the softer the pulp will become and the easier it will be to extract the remaining juice in Step 6. Stir the mixture two or three times each day during this soaking period. This gives the juice a chance to absorb more of the natural minerals and nutrients from the skin and pulp of the fruit. The yeast will feed on these nutrients during fermentation (Steps 14 through 18). Allowing the skins and pulp to mix with the juice will add flavor, color, and character to your final wine. Your finished wine will also retain its color and flavor for a longer period of time. If you wait six days you will notice a little foam on your juice and you sill see a few bubbles on top of the foam. This is the wild yeast in action.

6. **Straining and Juice Extraction:** Strain the liquid juice through a clean towel spread over the inside of a colander or strainer. Using a clean towel will make it easier to squeeze the fruit inside the towel and extract as much of the juice as possible. Save the juice. You may now discard the skins and pulp residue, or add them to your compost pile, or use them some other way.

7. **Optional Hydrometer Reading:** If you have a hydrometer then check the specific gravity (S.G.) and adjust it to between 1.085 to 1.105 by adding sugar or water as appropriate in Steps 8 and 9 below. If you don't have a hydrometer then simply follow the instructions in Steps 8 and 9 below.

8. **Optional Sugar** (highly desirable): If available add two-pounds (or four-cups) of sugar to one-quart (or four-cups) of boiling water. Stir the sugar until the sugar is completely dissolved in the water. Then turn off the heat and add two quarts of room temperature well water or spring water to the sugar solution and stir. Wait for the three quarts of sugar water to cool down to room temperature (75°F or 24°C) or below.

9. **Water:** If sugar water is available (Step 8) then add three quarts of room temperature sugar water to the juice. If sugar is not available then measure the juice and only add an equal amount of well water or spring water to the juice. The juice is called "must" at this stage.

10. **Optional Wild Yeast:** If you don't have any package yeast then you may use the natural wild yeast that was on the skins of your fruit or grapes or berries. You have approximately a 50% chance of capturing a good wine making yeast instead of some other wild yeast, such as a bread yeast. Randomly finding a good wine yeast is a win-or-lose proposition and you will only win about half the time. If you are using a wild yeast then skip Steps 11 and 12 below.

11. **Eliminating the Wild Yeast:** If you are using a wild yeast then immediately skip to Step 13. However, if you plan to use a package yeast then heat the juice to between 125°F to 135°F (or 52°C to 57°C) for five minutes. Do **not** boil the juice. The very low heat will kill any wild yeast that is present in the juice. Then turn off the heat and cover the pot to avoid contamination of the juice with any wild yeast floating in the air. Allow the juice to cool down to room temperature. (Note: Heating the juice **before** fermentation will **not** damage the final wine.) (Note: Instead of heating the juice you could add one crushed campden tablet per gallon of juice, cover the container with a towel, and let it stand for 24 hours. The campden tablet will kill any wild yeast in the juice so it cannot interact with your package yeast in Step 12 below.)

12. **Optional Package Yeast:** Dissolve one package of wine yeast (or bread yeast) in four-ounces of warm water (95°F to 105°F) (or 35°C to 40°C) that contains one-half teaspoon of sugar. Test the water on your wrist. It should feel warm but not hot. If the water is too hot it will kill the yeast. If the water is too cold it will slow down the process. Good yeast will become foamy and creamy after about 10 to 12 minutes. (Note: If the yeast does not foam after 15 minutes then the yeast is too old and it should not be used.) Mix the foamy yeast solution into the juice (now called "must") inside the large bucket or stock pot.

13. **Optional Yeast Nutrient or Yeast Energizer:** If available add 3/4 teaspoon of yeast nutrient or energizer into the juice and stir. Yeast nutrient, or DAP or Di-Ammonium Phosphate, is available at wine making shops and suppliers. The nutrient provides nitrogen and phosphorus for the yeast to consume as it makes alcohol. (Note: Yeast nutrient is preferred for grape wines and yeast energizer is preferred for fruit wines.) (Note: Well water and spring water both contain natural minerals and nutrients that the yeast can consume.)

14. **Yeast Multiplication:** Cover the pot with a towel to keep insects and flies out of the juice. Let the yeast multiply for five days inside the pot. The **yeast needs air** to successfully multiply during this five day period. The yeast is increasing in numbers and it needs air to reach a reasonable saturation level inside the liquid. If you shut off the air then the yeast will not be able to multiply and you will **not** end up with a good wine a year from now.

15. **Topping Off:** Pour the juice into a glass fermentation bottle or jug. If necessary add enough well water or spring water to reduce the air space in the top of the bottle to about two inches. This will minimize the impact of oxidation.

16. **Air Restriction:** Secure a 9-inch or 12-inch diameter balloon or an air-lock to the top of the jug. (Note: If you are using a new balloon then first inflate the balloon and then let the air out so the balloon will inflate more easily after it is on the wine jug.) The **yeast does not need air** during this stage. The yeast will feed on the minerals in the well water as it converts the sugar into alcohol and carbon dioxide. Place the jug in a cool dark area that is between 65°F to 75°F (or 18°C to 24°C). If the temperature is too low or too high then the fermentation process will slow down or stop. (Note: If you prefer to use an air-lock then remove the cap, pour a little clean water into the air-lock until it is half-full, and then insert the narrow end of the air-lock into a hole in the cork in the top of the bottle. The carbon dioxide will bubble up through the water trap and out the top of the air-lock.)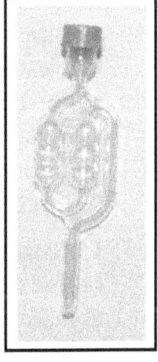

Chapter Thirty-Five: Wine

17. **Fermentation:** The balloon will gradually inflate due to the carbon dioxide (CO^2) that is formed during the natural fermentation process. Periodically gently loosen the bottom of the balloon, release the gas inside the balloon, and then re-secure the balloon back onto the jug. Do not completely remove the balloon from the jug. Try to avoid letting fresh air into the bottle as you release the carbon dioxide from inside the balloon. (Note: An air-lock does **not** need human intervention.)

18. **Fermentation Period:** Depending on a variety of factors, the fermentation process will normally take between one to six weeks if the temperature is between 65°F to 75°F (or 18°C to 24°C). When the balloon stops expanding and remains collapsed on top of the jug for two consecutive days (or there are no bubbles inside the air-lock for two days), then the fermentation process has stopped.

19. **Optional Step:** If you have a hydrometer then check the specific gravity of the wine. If it is 1.000 or less then the fermentation is complete. If you have a campden tablet then you may crush it and drop it into the wine at this time and wait 24 hours. The campden tablet will neutralize any remaining active yeast.

20. **Bottling the New Wine:** Siphon or very gently pour the "new wine" into storage bottles or jugs being very careful not to disturb the sediment (inactive yeast) on the bottom of the original jug. Pouring or filtering the wine through a new paper coffee filter will help to keep the wine clear and sediment free.

21. **New Wine Taste Test:** Taste test one spoonful of the "new wine." It will almost always taste bitter. Now is the time to add some sweetening "sugar water solution" to the wine.

22. **Sugar Water Solution:** Boil one-quarter cup of water and then gradually add one-half cup of sugar and stir. Continue to gently boil for about 5 minutes or until the sugar water solution looks clear. Wait for the solution to cool to 100°F (38°C) or less. Add one-half cup of this sugar water solution to each gallon of new wine. If you did **not** add the optional campden tablet in Step 19 then put a balloon on top of the bottle and wait 14 days. After 14 days, or when the balloon finally stops expanding, remove the balloon from the top of the bottle.

23. **Optional Raisins:** If available, add five raisins to each gallon of "new wine." The raisins will improve the final flavor of the future "aged wine."

24. **Corking:** Put a damp cork in the top of each bottle of "new wine."

25. **Aging:** Store the "new wine" in a cool dark place. Wait at least six to twelve months for the wine to age. The wine will continue to improve in flavor the longer it ages in a cool area. Good wines that have aged for three or four years are usually much better than wines that are only one year old. However, poor quality wines will not improve with age regardless of how long you wait.

26. **Aged Wine Taste Test:** Taste test one spoonful of the "aged wine." If the wine tastes bitter then add one-half cup of "sugar water solution" (see instructions at Step 22 above) to each gallon of aged wine and wait 24 hours and then taste the wine again. If the wine is still bitter then add another one-half cup of sugar water solution and taste again after 24 hours. If you used a "**standard wine yeast**" and the taste is still unacceptable then do not make wine using this particular type of fruit, grapes, or berries in the future. However, if you used a "**wild yeast**" then the unacceptable flavor of the "aged wine" could be due to the fact that you were not lucky and you did not have a good strain of wild yeast to begin with. Even if the wine does **not** have a superior flavor, it is still an alcoholic beverage and during hard times most people will not object to it since it will probably be the only alcoholic beverage available.

27. **Consumption:** If you succeed in making a good wine then enjoy your "aged wine" with a meal, or before or after a meal. (Note: Always comply with the legal "minimum drinking age" laws in your area.)

Grandpappy's Kudzu Flower Wine

6 quarts fresh kudzu blossoms
2 pounds sugar
1 package champagne or wine yeast (or bread yeast)
5 raisins per gallon (optional)
1 gallon well water or spring water

Pick kudzu blossoms when they are dry (mid-day). Rinse in running water to remove any foreign particles, dirt, or dust. Pour three quarts of boiling water over the blossoms and stir. Put a lid on the container and stir twice a day for four days.

Strain the liquid through a clean cloth. Press the blossoms to get all the liquid from them. Add four cups sugar. Dissolve yeast in lukewarm water. Pour the dissolved yeast into the liquid. Stir well. Cover and let it stand for five days. Transfer to a one-gallon jug. Add enough well water to bring the liquid within two inches below the top of the jug. Attach the balloon. Place jug in a cool dark place that is between 65°F to 75°F (18°C to 24°C). Periodically gently loosen the bottom of the balloon and allow the gas to escape. Then replace the balloon on the jug. In approximately six weeks the balloon will stop expanding and the wine is done. Strain the wine through a clean cloth or paper coffee filter and transfer it to airtight bottles. (Optional: Drop five raisins into each one-gallon bottle.) Cork tightly. Allow it to sit for an additional six to twelve months before drinking.

Grandpappy's Dandelion Flower Wine

2 quarts of dandelion flower petals (no tops, no stems, no leaves)
1 pound white sugar
1 pound light or dark brown sugar
1 package champagne or wine yeast (or bread yeast)
1/4 cup lemon juice (optional)
1/4 cup lime or grape juice (optional)
1/4 cup orange juice (optional)
5 raisins per gallon (optional)
1 gallon well water or spring water

Comment: Use a total of about 1/2 to 3/4 cup of any combination of juices, if available.
Comment: Use a total of 2 pounds of sugar, either white or brown or a combination of both.
Variation: Instead of the raisin use a small piece of fresh fig, apricot, apple, peach, or pear.

Pick dandelion flowers in the morning just before noon. The flowers should be fully open at that time. Pull the flower petals off the green part of the flower and only save the petals. Rinse the dandelion petals well. Boil three quarts of well water or spring water. Pour the boiling water over the dandelion flower petals and cover the pot. Let stand for four days. Stir twice a day. Strain to remove the flower petals (a coffee filter does a good job). Add the white and dark sugars, and the juices if available. Bring to a boil and boil for twenty minutes. Allow to cool gradually. Add the wine yeast when the water temperature is about 100°F (38°C), or when it feels comfortably warm to the back of your wrist. Cover and let it stand for five days. Pour into large glass bottles or jugs and attach a balloon to the top of each jug. Periodically gently loosen the bottom of the balloon and let the balloon deflate. After about two months, when the wine "falls clear," all the yeast and other particles will fall to the bottom of the bottle, and the wine will appear clear. Be patient and wait for your wine to clear by itself. Slowly and carefully transfer the clear wine to another bottle. (Optional: Drop five raisins into each one-gallon bottle.) Cork tightly. Let it stand for another six to twelve months in a cool, dark place.

Index

A
Abbreviations 1
Acorn Bread 71
Acorn Cookies 72
Acorn Grits 70
Acorn Meal 70
Acorn Muffins 71
Acorns 64
Alcohol 91
Aluminum 3
Apple Cake 41
Armadillo 79

B
Baby Formula 89
Bacon 4
Bagels 31
Baked Rice 14
Baking Powder 1,3,5
Baking Powder Biscuits 25
Baking Soda 3
Barley 93
Bark, Tree 59
Beans 11,13,18
Bear 81
Beaver 79
Beef Broth 18
Beer 91
Beets, Sugar 9
Berries 58
Beverages 89
Birch Juice 59
Biscuits 25,26,27,30
Bisquick 3
Blueberry Crisp 50
Blueberry Pudding 56
Bone Marrow 82
Bread on the Grill 24
Bugs 77
Buns, Sandwich 22
Burrito 13
Butter 21
Buttermilk 1,21
Butterscotch Candy 53

C
Cake 41
Candy 51
Caramel 43,53
Caramel Popcorn 55
Caramel Syrup 55
Catsup 8
Cattails 58
Celsius 2
Centigrade 2
Cereal, Wheat Berry 36,37
Cheese Crackers 32
Cheese Wafers 32
Chicken and Dumplings 17
Chicken Broth 17
Chicken Fried Steak 17
Chili with Beans 19
Chips, Corn 34
Chips, Potato 12
Chips, Whole Wheat 32
Chocolate Cake 41,42
Chocolate Milk, Milkshake 89
Chocolate Fudge 52
Chocolate Pudding 56
Choctaw Indian Fry Bread 27
Cinnamon 43
Cinnamon Rolls 54
Clover 59
Clover Tea 90
Cobbler 49
Cocoa Fudge 52,53
Cookies 44
Coon 80
Corn Chips 34
Corn Cob Jelly 57
Corn Dogs 35
Cornmeal 34
Cornmeal Mush 35
Corn Pone 34
Crackers 31,32
Crayfish 77
Crescent Cookies 44
Crescent Rolls 23
Crust Variations 20

D
Daisy 59
Dandelions 60
Dandelion Wine 101
Deer 81
Dutch Cookies 45

E
E. Coli (Escherichia) 88
Eggs 4,20,21
Electrolyte Beverage 89
English Muffin Loaf 24
English Muffins 23
Evergreen Needles 59

F
Fahrenheit 2
Fantastic Fudge 53
Feathered Rice 13
Fish 76
Flour, Self-Rising 5
French Bread 22,28
Fried Pies 50
Fried Rice 16
Frogs 77
Frostings 42,43
Fruit Cobbler 49,50
Fruit Pectin 6
Fruit Preserves Cookies 44
Fruit Preserves Pie 49
Fruit Salad 16
Fudge 52

G
Gatorade 89
Glazed Acorn Treats 72
Graham Crackers 31
Graham Cracker Pie Crust 49
Granola 35,57
Grasshoppers 77
Griddlecakes, Acorn 70
Groundhog 79

H
Hamburger, Rice, and Eggs 15
Hard Cake 41
Hash, Roast Beef 18
Hash Browns 12
Herb Flavored Rice 14
Hickory Nut Cake 74
Hickory Nut Pie 75
Hoe Cakes 35
Honey 21
Honey Cookies 46
Hops 93
Hop Yeast 6

Hot Chocolate 89
Huckleberry Crisp 50
Hush Puppies 34

I
Ice Cream 40
Icings 41,43,54
Indian Acorn Griddlecakes 70
Indian Fry Bread 27
Indian Pemmican 85
Indian Rice 14
Irish Soda Bread 27

J
Jelly, Corn Cob 57
Jerky, Meat 83

K
Ketchup, Catsup 8
Kudzu 62
Kudzu Wine 101

L
Lamb's Quarters 59
Liquid Substitutions 21
Liquor, Whiskey 92
Listeria Monocytogenesis 88
Loaf Bread 22

M
Mackerel Patties 19
Marshmallows 55
Mayonnaise 5
Meatballs 19
Meat Grinder 82
Meat Jerky 83
Mexican Acorn Tortillas 70
Mexican Rice 14
Mexican Salsa 8
Milk, Condensed 5
Milk, Instant Nonfat Dry 3
Milkshakes 89
Muffins, English 23,24
Muskrat 79

N
Navaho Indian Fry Bread 27
Northern Fried Chicken 17
Nutrition 38,60,63,73,75

O

Oak Trees	64
Oat Flour	33
Oatmeal Bread	33
Oatmeal Cookies	47
Opossum	79

P

Pancakes	25,30,71
Parched Corn	35
Peanut Butter	6,43
Peanut Butter Balls	54
Peanut Butter Candy	51
Peanut Butter Cookies	54
Peanut Butter Fudge	52
Peanut Butter Milkshake	89
Pear Preserves	57
Pecan Sandies	46
Pectin	6
Pedialyte	89
Pemmican	85
Pemmican Tortilla	70
Pepper	1
Pie Crusts	48
Pine Needles	59
Pinole	35
Pioneer Acorn Bread	71
Pioneer Acorn Pancakes	71
Pioneer Hoe Cakes	34
Pioneer Pudding	56
Pita Bread	24
Pizza Crust	24
Pizza Sauce	8
Poke Sallet Weed	61
Polenta	35
Popped Corn, Popcorn	55
Popped Wheat	37
Porcupine	80
Potato Cakes	12
Potato Chips	12
Potato Water	21
Pot Luck Pie	16
Preserves, Pear	57
Pretzels	31
Pudding	56

Q

Quantity Conversion Table	1

R

Rabbit	80
Raccoon	80
Refried Beans	11
Rice	13
Rice Adjunct, Beer	93
Rice-A-Roni	15
Rice Beverage	89
Rice Flour	13,33
Rice Milkshake	89
Rice Pilaf	15
Rice Pudding	57
Rice Sundae	57
Roast Beef Hash	18
Rockahominy	35
Rolls, Crescent	23
Rolls, Hard	23
Russian Tea	90

S

Salad, Wheat Berry	37
Salmonella	88
Salmon Patties	19
Salsa	8
Salt	1,21
Salt-Rising Bread	26
Sandwich Buns	22
Sausage and Cheese Biscuits	27
Scones	27,45
Scottish Butter Cookies	45
Scrambled Eggs	4
Shish Kabobs or Kebabs	18
Shoo Fly Pie	49
Shortbread Cookies	44
Shortcake	41
Snails	77
Snakes	77
Snowball Cookies	46
Sour Cream	5
Sourdough Bread	29
Sourdough French Bread	30
Sourdough Starter	28,29
Southern Fried Chicken	17
Southern Pastry	48
Spaghetti with Meat Balls	19
Spaghetti Sauce	7
Spam	14,16,18
Spanish Rice	14

Spirits, Liquor 92
Sprouts 36,37
Squirrel 80
Staphylococcus Aureus 88
Stuffed Grape Leaves 15
Substitutions 1
Substitutions, Liquid 21
Sugar Beets 9,98
Sugar Cookies 44
Sugar, Homemade 9
Swedish Butter Cookies 45
Sweet Rice 16
Sweet Sticky Buns 54

T
Taco Shells 34
Tannic Acid 67
Tea 59,63,90
Temperature Conversion Chart 2
Three Grain Bread 33
Tomato Sauce 7
Tortillas 13,25,27,34,70
Tree Bark 59
Trout 76
Tuna 16,18
Turtles 77

U
Unsweetened Chocolate 1

V
Venison, Deer 81
Vienna Sausages 18,35

W
Welch Scones 45
Wheat Berries 21,36
Wheat Berry Cereal 36
Wheat Berry Nutrition Data 39
Wheat Berry Salad 37
Wheat Sprouts 36,37
Whiskey 92
White Rice 13
Wieners 18
Wild Game Processing 78
Wild Game Stew 82
Wild Plants, Edible 58
Wild Plants, Safety 58
Wine 59,91,97
Woodchuck 79

X

Y
Yeast, Beer 95
Yeast, Bread 20
Yeast, Wine 97
Yeast, Hop 6

About the Author

Robert Wayne Atkins, P.E. (Grandpappy)

Born in 1949. Accepted Jesus Christ as Savior in April of 1976.

B.S. Degree in Industrial Engineering & Operations Research, Virginia Polytechnic Institute and State University, Blacksburg, Virginia, June 1972.

Master of Business Administration, Major in Marketing, Georgia State University, Atlanta, Georgia, March 1985.

Licensed Professional Engineer (P.E.), Florida 1980, Georgia 1982.

Ordained Deacon in Christian Church, Ocala, Florida, 1980.

Member of The Gideons International continuously since 1979.

Author of Nine Computer Software Games, including "**The Lost Crown of Queen Anne,**" 1988-1991.

Contributing Author to "**Maynard's Industrial Engineering Handbook,**" 5th Edition, p. 5.10, 2001.

Contributing Author to "**Maynard's Industrial & Systems Engineering Handbook**" 6th Edition, p. 102, 2023.

Listed in "**Who's Who in America,**" 64th Edition, 2010.

Listed in "**Who's Who in the World,**" 29th Edition, 2012.

Recipient of "**Who's Who**" Lifetime Achievement Award, 2019.

Picture Taken in 2004.
Grandpappy Age 55.

Robert is a descendant of the early European settlers in Virginia who married American Indian Cherokee wives.

In the year 2003 Robert began writing down what he had learned from the Holy Bible after more than 25 years of reading it on a daily basis. But he suspected his children might not read what he wrote if he put it into a sermon format. Therefore he began writing short Christian poems because he hoped that his children, grandchildren, and his other future descendants might take the time to read a short poem even if it was Christian oriented.

Later it occurred to him that some of his knowledge might be of interest to other people. Therefore he began publishing some of his writings on his website. Based on the favorable email feedback he received he continued to freely share his knowledge on his website. After several years, and at the request of many of his readers, he eventually consolidated some of his writings into the books below.

Other Books by this Same Author:

1. Handbook of Industrial, Systems, and Quality Engineering (English and Spanish).
2. Introduction to Engineering Management.
3. Engineering Statistics and Applications.
4. Engineering Economy and Financial Analysis.
5. Introduction to Quality Engineering.
6. Introduction to Industrial and Systems Engineering (and Instructor's Manual).
7. Work Measurement and Ergonomics (and Instructor's Manual).
8. Facilities Design and Plant Layout (and Instructor's Manual).
9. Practical Small-Scale Electrical Energy Systems.
10. Practical Strategies for Long-Term Survival.
11. The Practical Prepper's Survival Handbook.
12. Self-Defense Weapons: Traditional and Modern.
13. How to Maximize Your Eating Pleasure and Your Life Expectancy.
14. The Common Sense Diet.
15. The Food Book.
16. Grandpappy's Gourmet Cookbook.
17. Grandpappy's Campfire Survival Cookbook (English and Spanish).
18. Grandpappy's Survival Manual for Hard Times, Third Edition.
19. The Most Important Survival Skills of the 1800s.
20. How to Tan Animal Hides and How to Make High Quality Buckskin Clothing.
21. How to Live Comfortably for Several Years in a Hostile Wilderness Environment.
22. The New Heaven and The New Earth (English and Spanish).
23. Some Difficult Questions Answered Using the Holy Bible.
24. Religion and Christianity in the Twenty-First Century.
25. Grandpappy's Christian Poems.
26. Grandpappy's Stories for Children of All Ages.
27. Ancient Board Games and Solitaire Games from Around the World.
28. The Four Pillars of Prosperity: Governments, Businesses, Religions, and Banks.

www.ingramcontent.com/pod-product-compliance
Lightning Source LLC
Chambersburg PA
CBHW081458040426
42446CB00016B/3302